LIVING
INDIANA
HISTORY

HEARTLAND OF AMERICA

Editorial Director:
Hubert H. Hawkins,
Secretary, Indiana Historical Society

Executive Editor and Educational Consultant:
Leo C. Fay,
Indiana University, Bloomington

Authors:
Eth Clifford   Richard E. Kirk   James N. Rogers

*Illustrated by David Kinney
and Creative Designs Studios*

DAVID-STEWART PUBLISHING COMPANY, INC.
INDIANAPOLIS, INDIANA

ACKNOWLEDGMENT

The authors and editors of *Living Indiana History* have endeavored to present an accurate, balanced and exciting account of Indiana's development in both text and illustration. Basic social studies concepts are integrated in the historical narrative. Essential data from American and world history has been interwoven with the Indiana story. We wish gratefully to acknowledge the invaluable assistance generously supplied by:

RICHARD CALDMEYER, *Ball State University, Muncie*
MISS CAROLINE DUNN, *Indiana Historical Society Library*
JAMES KELLAR, *Indiana University, Bloomington*
MRS. JOHN McKAY, *Indianapolis Public Schools*
MISS NORMA E. PHILLIPS, *Indianapolis Public Schools*
DONALD SCHEICK, *Indiana State University, Terre Haute*
HARRY M. SMITH, *Connersville Public Schools*

Full responsibility for the text however, rests entirely with the authors and editors.

Leo C. Fay
Executive Editor and Educational Consultant

Hubert H. Hawkins
Editorial Director

Authors: ETH CLIFFORD, RICHARD E. KIRK, JAMES N. ROGERS

CONTENTS

U. S. 1533159

If Indiana were painted white it would look like this white dot.
Do you live in Indiana? Then you are somewhere inside this dot!

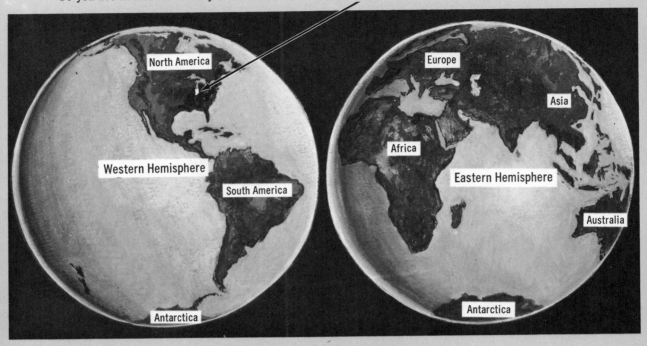

North America

Europe

Asia

Africa

Western Hemisphere

Eastern Hemisphere

South America

Australia

Antarctica

Antarctica

This is the planet Earth. If you were in a space ship flying toward our world, the earth might look like one of these halves. The two halves on the map are called the Eastern and Western Hemispheres.

The continents of North and South America are in the Western Hemisphere. Indiana is on the continent of North America.

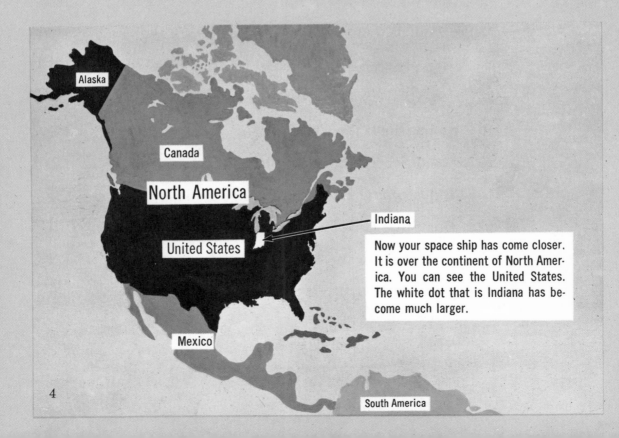

Alaska

Canada

North America

Indiana

United States

Now your space ship has come closer. It is over the continent of North America. You can see the United States. The white dot that is Indiana has become much larger.

Mexico

South America

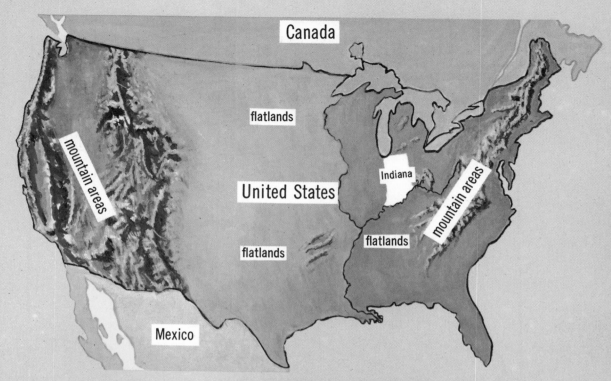

Your space ship is flying over the United States. This map shows where the mountains and flatlands are. You can see the shape of Indiana now.

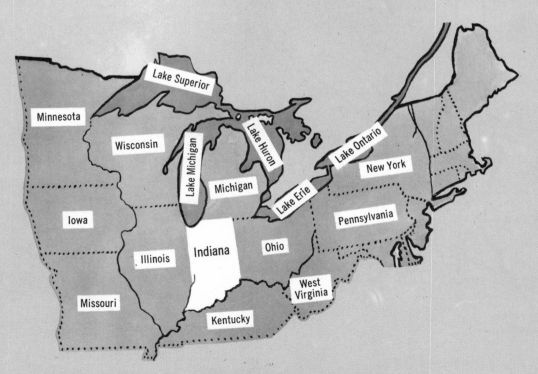

Your space ship is ready to land. You are in Indiana. Now you can begin to learn the exciting story of your state.

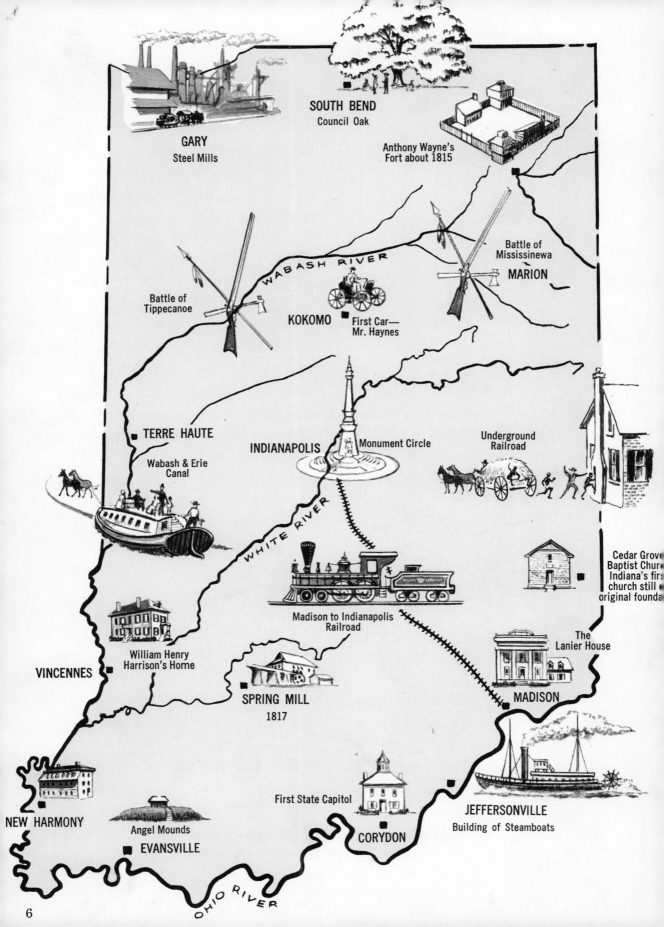

GARY
Steel Mills

SOUTH BEND
Council Oak

Anthony Wayne's
Fort about 1815

Battle of
Mississinewa

MARION

Battle of
Tippecanoe

KOKOMO   First Car—
Mr. Haynes

WABASH RIVER

TERRE HAUTE

INDIANAPOLIS   Monument Circle

Underground
Railroad

Wabash & Erie
Canal

WHITE RIVER

Cedar Grove
Baptist Chur
Indiana's firs
church still
original founda

Madison to Indianapolis
Railroad

The
Lanier House

William Henry
Harrison's Home

VINCENNES

SPRING MILL
1817

MADISON

NEW HARMONY

Angel Mounds

EVANSVILLE

First State Capitol

CORYDON

JEFFERSONVILLE
Building of Steamboats

OHIO RIVER

6

1

Indiana—A Place on the Map

Before There Was an Indiana

Indiana is a state. It is one of the fifty states that make up our country. But once there was no Indiana. There wasn't even a United States of America. Nor was there any other country. States and countries were made by men. So until man thought of dividing land into parts, states and countries did not exist. But the land itself did exist. The place we call Indiana has been here a long, long time.

When someone talks about the history of a place, he usually means the history of that place after it was named by men. He is talking about the time that has passed since that place was marked off, put on a map and called by a name.

But the history of a place also can mean something else. It can mean all the time that has passed since the land was first formed as part of the young earth. The history of what happened to the land, even before man lived on it and named it, is called geologic (jē-ə-lŏj′ĭk) history. The history of man living on the land is called cultural history. Both kinds of history are important, because they both help us understand how things came to be as they are now.

Man is a maker of lines. He draws some lines around his house and says, "The land inside these lines is my yard." He draws other lines and says, "The land inside the lines is my town." Or he draws lines and says, "The land inside is my state." Of course, he doesn't draw the lines on the land itself. He makes a picture of the land and makes lines on the picture. He calls the picture with lines on it a map.

Maps Tell a Story

A map may be of a town, a state, a nation or even of the whole earth. A map shows the land divided into parts and the names man has given to those parts.

So Indiana is the name given to a particular place. The land we call Indiana was always part of the North American continent. Only no one could tell Indiana from any other place until some men made a map that showed what part of the land would be called Indiana.

Today, Indiana can be found on

any map of the United States. A map of the state itself will have lines that divide the land into still smaller parts. These smaller parts are called counties. Counties, too, are divided into smaller parts called townships. And within townships there are towns or cities. All these areas of land have been marked off and given names by men.

A map may show other things too. It may show high places and low places, hills and flatlands. It may show streams, rivers, lakes and forests. Man did not make rivers, lakes and hills. He simply measured them and made maps to show where and what they were.

Not all maps show the land as it is today. By studying the land today, men have been able to tell what it was like in the past. Some maps show how the land looked millions of years ago. They may even show what happened in the past to change the land.

Every map tells a special story. Maps are the tools men use to show how they have divided the land. They are tools men use to show the history of the land.

The maps in this book are tools that help us understand the story of the land we call Indiana. They are tools that help us understand the story of the men who explored, settled and divided the land.

What This Book Will Tell You

This book tells the story of how Indiana came to be. It tells the story of the land before men had yet appeared on the earth. It tells why the land is as it is today. It tells why there are rolling hills and lakes in one place and flat grasslands somewhere else. There are maps that help us understand that part of the story.

This book also tells the story of what men have done. It tells the story of the men who drew lines and called the land inside the lines Indiana. It tells the story of the people who have lived in Indiana. It tells what the people have done and what they are doing now. Much of this story, too, can be seen in maps.

So Indiana is a place on the map. But to find out just how it came to be, one must go back a long, long way. One must go back to the time before man had yet appeared on earth. One must go back to the time when the land was still being formed. That is really the beginning of the story of Indiana.

Chapter 2...How the Age of Ice Changed Indiana

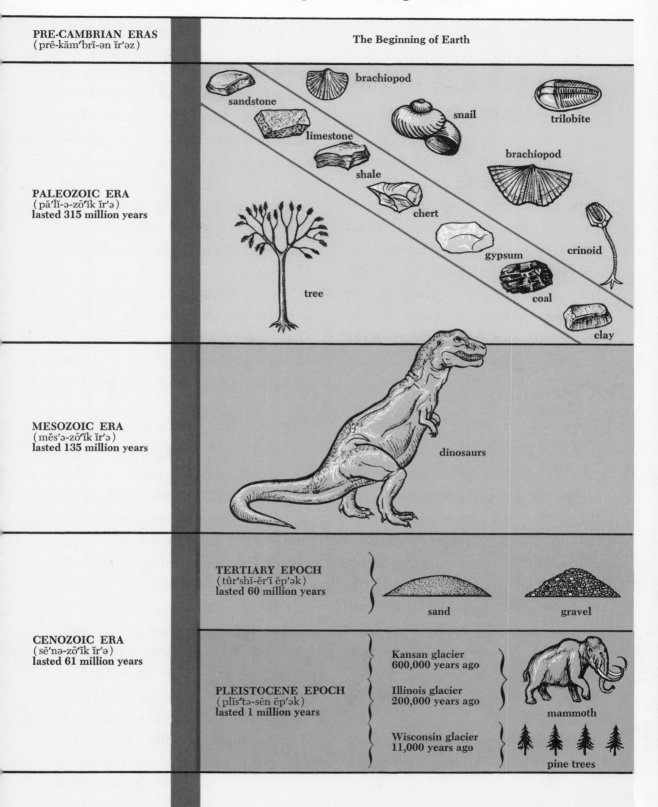

PRE-CAMBRIAN ERAS
(prē-kăm′brĭ-ən ĭr′əz)

The Beginning of Earth

PALEOZOIC ERA
(pā′lĭ-ə-zō′ĭk ĭr′ə)
lasted 315 million years

sandstone

brachiopod

limestone

snail

trilobite

shale

brachiopod

chert

gypsum

crinoid

tree

coal

clay

MESOZOIC ERA
(mĕs′ə-zō′ĭk ĭr′ə)
lasted 135 million years

dinosaurs

TERTIARY EPOCH
(tûr′shĭ-ĕr′ĭ ĕp′ək)
lasted 60 million years

sand

gravel

CENOZOIC ERA
(sē′nə-zō′ĭk ĭr′ə)
lasted 61 million years

PLEISTOCENE EPOCH
(plĭs′tə-sēn ĕp′ək)
lasted 1 million years

Kansan glacier
600,000 years ago

Illinois glacier
200,000 years ago

mammoth

Wisconsin glacier
11,000 years ago

pine trees

9

2

How the Age of Ice Changed Indiana

Indiana is in the Midwestern part of the United States. Scientists know that long ago a great part of the Midwestern United States was covered by a sea.

We know what kinds of sea animals and sea plants lived in the Midwest millions of years ago by the fossils (fŏs′əlz) they left. Even today in Indiana, fossils may be found in lime and sandstone.

How the Earth Changed

Very slowly, as time went on, a part of the Midwest was raised above the water by pressure inside the earth. And just as slowly, some of the water animals changed to animals with legs and lungs. These animals, called reptiles and amphibians (ăm-fĭb′ĭ-ənz), began to spend a part of their lives on land. Some of the water plants also began to live on the land. Other kinds of water plants and animals just died out.

Finally, there came a time when almost all the Midwest was land. And some of the land plants and land animals had changed even more. Now, there were birds, insects and trees as well as land animals, reptiles and amphibians.

All the time that plants and animals were changing and land was rising above the drying seas, pressures were working under the earth. The pressures pushed the land up in certain places. Then, hills and valleys formed in the Midwest.

Today, there are hills and valleys only in the southern part of Indiana. The great change in most of Indiana's land was made by huge, thick sheets of ice called glaciers.

The Age of Ice Begins

About one million years ago, the first of the great glaciers formed in the northern part of the North American continent. The area where the glacier formed is known today as Canada. Scientists call the time of the great glaciers "The Age of Ice."

Very slowly, the first glacier built itself up from billions of tons of Canadian snow. The snow became packed into heavy ice by its own great weight. As the glacier became thicker and heavier with each Canadian snowfall, it began to spread like pancake batter in a

The glaciers melted before they reached the hills of southern Indiana

frying pan. But the high wall of the first glacier melted before it reached the Midwest.

The Illinois Glacier

Then, another glacier formed. This glacier is called the Illinois glacier. The Illinois glacier covered much of Indiana. The Illinois glacier spread very slowly. In one place, it moved only 1½ inches each day. That is a speed of one mile every 115 years!

The Wisconsin Glacier

The last glacier to enter Indiana is called the Wisconsin glacier. It did not reach much below the center of the state before it melted away.

As a result of the glaciers that reached the Midwest, Indiana has two very different land surfaces. The northern half of Indiana is almost flat, as it was leveled by the glaciers.

But parts of southern Indiana are still very hilly, as none of the glaciers reached those places.

One area, just fifty miles below Indianapolis, has the same steep hills it had before the Age of Ice. Most of this area is in Brown County, which has some of the most beautiful hills and valleys in the Midwest. In the fall, when Indiana's leaves change from green to yellow and red, thousands of people drive to see the steep hills and valleys of Brown County wrapped in beautiful colors.

How the Land Was Changed

The glaciers changed Indiana's land surface in many different ways. For example, as the glaciers moved down from Canada, they tore away many rocks and boulders and carried these with them. Rocks can cut and scrape, as you know if you have ever fallen on gravel. Pressed down by millions of tons of glacial ice, the rocks and boulders cut and scraped their way over northern Indiana's land surface.

Another thing the glaciers did was to push much of Canada's rich, black soil into Indiana. When they melted, the glaciers left much of this rich soil in the north central part of Indiana. And that is why the north central part of Indiana is such good farmland today. No better corn or tomatoes grow anywhere in the world than in north central Indiana.

The New Rivers

Scientists call the rocks, boulders, soil, sand and gravel "glacial drift." Indiana's glacial drift even contained a few diamonds, which have been found in Morgan County and in Brown County. Boys and girls living in those two counties should keep their eyes open for these gems.

Before the glaciers moved into the Midwest, many Indiana rivers flowed north instead of south, as most do today. A million years ago, the Teays (Tāz) River flowed north into Ohio and Indiana from its beginning in the Blue Ridge Mountains of Virginia. And instead of the great river that it is today, the Mississippi River was just a small north-flowing branch of the Teays River.

Today, the Teays River is gone, and the Mississippi River flows south into the Gulf of Mexico. The glaciers buried the Teays and turned the Mississippi southward.

The strength of the glaciers against the rivers played one more great part in the Midwest's geo-

Glacial drift

logic history. As the glaciers stopped the northward flow of the rivers, some of the river waters began to spread out. The waters sometimes spread out around the edges of the glaciers that blocked their flow. The spreading waters began to form small lakes. Then, when the glaciers melted away, they added their waters to the lakes, making them larger. The five Great Lakes, which began as dry, low places north of Indiana, were formed in this way.

When the melting glaciers poured so much of their water on Indiana's land, the rivers helped carry much of the water away. But some of the water stayed on the land to form swamps. Now, most of the large swamps are gone. They have been drained by ditches that men have dug. The ditches were dug from the swamps to the rivers, so that the swamp waters drained into the rivers. Because of its rivers, most of Indiana's good soil is well drained today.

Indiana's rivers gave early explorers and settlers a way into Indiana. The French explorer La Salle, the first white man to enter Indiana, paddled up the winding St. Joseph River that flows into Lake Michigan. Later, many of the first settlers in Indiana came here by boat. They traveled down rivers to the Ohio River, the southern boundary of Indiana. Then, they had only to step ashore to be in what would later become the state of Indiana.

As glacial ice melted, it often happened that huge blocks of ice were buried beneath glacial drift. As these blocks of ice melted, their water filled the holes they were in. In such a way, these holes became the hundreds of small northern Indiana lakes that so many Hoosiers enjoy in the summer.

Indiana Changes

After the last glacier melted, the weather in Indiana became close to what it is today. The sun warmed the land, and the rain watered the forests. Winters then, as now, were not too long or too cold. The soil and growing season would later be good for plants and crops.

Some of Indiana's important minerals were formed before the Age of Ice. Coal, gravel and building limestone are some of these minerals.

This, then, was how the Age of Ice changed Indiana. This was what the land of Indiana was like before the coming of man.

13

Chapter 3 . . . How the Ancient Indians Lived on Our Land

20,000 B.C. to A.D. 500	Prehistoric Indian history begins when men come across the Bering Straight
7000 B.C. to 5000 B.C.	Prehistoric Indians come to Indiana
500 B.C. to A.D. 500	The Shell Mound Indians
A.D. 500 to A.D. 900	The Adena Indians
A.D. 900 to A.D. 1300	The Hopewell Indians
A.D. 1300 to A.D. 1600	The Middle Mississippi Indians
A.D. 1550 to A.D. 1700	The Fort Ancient Indians
A.D. 1679	Historic Indian history begins when Robert de La Salle comes to Indiana

Fifty-six miles of sea separate Asia from Alaska.

3

How the Ancient Indians Lived on our Land

The Bridge to the New Land

For thousands of years before man began to write down the happenings of his time, there were no people in America. If the wind blew, or rainbows came after storms, or snow covered the earth, there was no one to see it or tell it.

But there were people in other parts of the world. Some lived in Europe. Others lived in Asia. These men were the Stone Age people. We call them Stone Age people because most of the tools and weapons that have survived from that time were made of stone. But archaeologists (är'kĭ-ŏl'ə-jəsts) now know that other materials were used by the Stone Age people, too.

No one is sure just how these early men wandered from the lands they knew to find our unexplored continent. But scientists believe that these people moved farther and farther north on the continent of Asia as they searched for food. And so one day they came to a place that led them to the new world of America.

Today, about fifty-six miles of sea separate the mainland of Alaska from the mainland of Asia. At its narrowest point, this sea is called the Bering Strait. The Bering Strait can be crossed either by ship or by airplane. But when the Stone

Age men stood on the mainland of Asia, and looked across to Alaska, there was a natural land bridge over which they could cross. When the first Stone Age men crossed the land bridge, the history of the prehistoric Indians began.

The First Stone Age People in America

For thousands of years after these first people crossed over, others continued to come after them. They came in small groups to this new-found land. Some stayed in Alaska. Others went on

to look for new and better hunting grounds.

All of these early people disappeared without leaving any written records behind them. When the white men first came to North America, there were only about 1,000,000 Indians spread out over all this vast land. And these Indians knew little or nothing about the prehistoric men who had roamed the land before them.

During the thousands of years in which the migrations of the Stone Age people took place, many changes came about in the land, in the climate, and in the people.

About 10,000 B.C., the climate in Indiana was cold and wet. There were many thick evergreen forests. But after 2,000 years, the climate began to change. The weather became less cold and not so wet. Now the forests had a number of other kinds of trees, too.

By about 1,000 B.C., the weather in Indiana had become quite warm and dry. It is thought to have been warmer and dryer than now. There were many grasslands, and oak and hickory trees grew in great number.

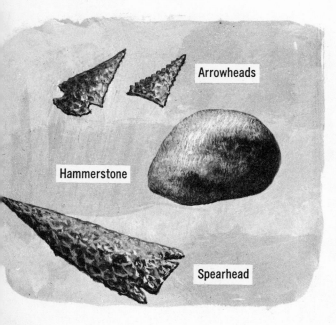

Arrowheads

Hammerstone

Spearhead

Important Tools Made By The Ancient Indians

Although no written records were left behind by the ancient Indians, archaeologists are able to tell a little about these early men from artifacts. Pottery, tools, spearheads and other things which have been discovered buried in the earth are called artifacts.

One artifact that seems to have been used from man's earliest days is the hammerstone. It was one of the ancient Indian's most important tools, for he could do many different things with it.

A hammerstone was used for cracking open bones and shells and nuts. With the hammerstone, food like seeds and roots could be ground very fine. It was a handy tool for shaping rocks into arrowheads and spearheads. The hammerstone was also used as a weapon in hunting and in fighting.

Prehistoric man used animal bones to make fishhooks and needles and other tools. From stone, he made arrow points, spearheads and pipes. He made pottery, too, such as round-bottom jars and bowls. Some jars and bowls were decorated with the figures of animals and humans.

The Shell Mound Indians

The ancient people who roamed over Indiana were mostly hunters and fishermen. The women gathered nuts and berries while the men hunted.

When the hunters and fishermen settled down, even for a short time, they usually camped near rivers. Here they caught shellfish in the White River, the Ohio River and the Wabash River.

After they took the meat from the shell, they threw the shells into a pile. Slowly the piles grew higher and higher. Archaeologists have discovered tools among the shells.

The Shell Mound Indians were rovers who moved from one place to another in search of food. They did not build permanent houses. Caves were used as shelters, or small huts that were easily thrown up and just as easily pulled down. They lived mostly in southern Indiana.

These early people were called the Shell Mound Indians because of the shell mounds found wherever these people lived. From digging in these mounds, archaeologists can tell us many interesting things about these people. They tell us, for example, that the Shell Mound Indians heated liquid for cooking by dropping hot rocks into the liquid. The cooking containers were usually made from animal skins, though they were sometimes made of wood or bark.

They were skillful at making other things. They not only made tools from the bones of animals, but ornaments to wear as well. Ornamental pins have been found in some of the mounds that the Shell Mound Indians cut from bone, polished and carved with different designs.

The Adena Indians

Other early people were also mound builders. But there was a big difference between these In-dians and the Shell Mound Indians. The Shell Mound Indians made careless piles out of things they did not need. The Indians who came after them built mounds of earth on purpose. Their mounds were used to bury their great chiefs and war-riors. And they were used, too, as places of worship. Their mounds didn't just happen. They were care-fully built.

These early woodland Indians, who came after the Shell Mound Indians, settled down in small villages. The first of these wood-land Indians lived in Indiana from 800 B.C., to A.D. 200 or 300. What they called themselves is not known but scientists named them the Adena (ə-dē'nə) Indians.

The houses in their villages were round and were made from branches and bark. Log poles held up the roofs and walls. The houses were put up near one another. It is believed that when some of the Indians died, the others burned the houses and built mounds over them. These people, like the Shell Mound Indians before them, stayed close to rivers, too.

The Hopewell Indians

The next group to appear in In-diana were called the Hopewell

Bone fishhook

Bone needle

Bone necklace

Indians. They appeared in Indiana about A.D. 200 to 500. These tribes seemed to have more skills than the people who came before them.

Like the Adena Indians, the Hopewell Indians built burial mounds, too. But they also built earth walls. These walls may have been put up to protect the villages from other warlike tribes. But it is believed that many of these walls set off areas that were used on important religious holidays. The walls had many different shapes. Some were built in squares or circles. Others were formed to look like animals.

The Hopewell Indians knew about copper, for they made many ornaments with this metal. The copper they used came from as far north as Michigan. They also used obsidian (ŏb-sĭd'ĭ-ən), which is a kind of glass found in rock and which came from the Rockies, and mica, a mineral which came from North Carolina.

The Hopewell Indians were farmers, as well as hunters and traders. They had small farms and gardens, in which they grew such crops as corn, squash and beans. They even grew tobacco, which they smoked in their unusual carved stone pipes.

They knew something about sav-ing for the harsh winter days when food was scarce. Pits were dug where food was stored for use in the winter.

The Middle Mississippi Indians

Now there came a group of people who had advanced in agriculture far beyond the earlier Indian tribes. They lived in southwestern Indiana. Like the other Indians before them, they too settled near the rivers. These Middle Mississippi Indians, as they have been named, had large villages around which were built walls of logs and earth.

These Indians seem to have used furniture in their homes. The furniture was no more than a simple bench, which was used both for sitting and sleeping. But they tried to make their homes more attractive and comfortable. And they also built a special home and temple for their chief, on top of one of the mounds.

The villages were planned carefully. They were set up around a large, open piece of flat ground, which was used for tribal dances and ceremonies.

These Indians planned their mounds just as carefully as they

planned their villages. All of the mounds had flat tops. The best example of these mounds in Indiana are the Angel Mounds near Evansville, Indiana. At least eleven mounds were built at this site. Archaeologists have found the remains of what seem to be temples, or large houses, on top of two of the mounds. One mound is more than forty feet high, 300 feet wide and 600 feet long.

These people seemed to live better than the Indian tribes who came before them. The benches they made were placed against the walls. In the center of the houses, fire pits were dug which served for cooking and heating. Pits found outside the houses were probably used to store grain for the winter.

The Middle Mississippi Indians may have had many enemies, for they surrounded their villages with strong walls. Some of the walls were at least a mile long, and often as high as fifteen feet.

Artifacts dug up from the Angel Mounds show that these Indians were skilled workmen. Other artifacts show that they tried to make things they used more beautiful.

They must have enjoyed music, for flutes made of bone were found in the village. And they must have invented games to play, for dice made out of bone were also discovered.

These Middle Mississippi Indians seem to have been a hard-working people, who tried to bring beauty and interest into their everyday lives.

The Fort Ancient Indians

The last of the prehistoric Indians to live in Indiana were the Fort Ancient tribes, who lived in southern and eastern Indiana. We know that like the Hopewell and the Middle Mississippi Indians, these Fort Ancient people farmed the land. Like the Middle Mississippi Indians, these Indians hunted, using the bow and arrow.

The houses of the Fort Ancient Indians were not all built alike. Some houses were round. Others had four sides. Skins, bark or mats were used to cover the houses.

Like the Middle Mississippi Indians, the Fort Ancient Indians seem to have enjoyed music. Archaeologists have discovered some musical instruments where their villages once stood.

Mounds built by the prehistoric Indians may still be seen today in state parks. The Mounds State Park is located at Anderson, Indiana. The Angel Mounds, made by the Middle Mississippi Indians, can be seen near Evansville, in southern Indiana.

The Jigsaw Puzzle

Trying to piece together the story of these early people is like working on a jigsaw puzzle, with some of the important pieces missing. Without written records, it is difficult to know the whole story of a people. But archaeologists have been able to learn a great deal about the ancient Indians from artifacts, mounds and villages buried in the earth.

We know that the Fort Ancient Indians, the Middle Mississippi Indians and the other prehistoric Indians stayed in Indiana for a time. They then seemed to disappear. But they did not just vanish from the scene. As times change, people change, too.

For example, there was a time in American history when people traveled by horse and buggy. Then cars were invented, and the horse and buggy was not fast enough for the changing times. Men once sailed the seas in clipper ships. Then fast steamers replaced the clipper ships.

Archaeologists tell us that for the ancient Indians, times and customs changed, too. The ancient Indians may have met with and married into other tribes. Slowly other and new ways may have taken the place of old ways. When the ancient Indians lived in a new way, it was like changing from the horse and buggy way of living to the way of life we now have with cars and airplanes.

When the white men came to America, they found Indians living here. These Indians knew nothing of the prehistoric men who had lived on the land before them. Archaeologists believe the prehistoric men came generally from the same race, and that the Indians the white men saw were descended from the prehistoric Indians.

Historic Indians of Indiana

The first known white men to enter Indiana were Robert de La Salle, a French explorer, and his followers. When they came to Indiana, they found the Miami Indians, as well as other tribes, living along the Wabash River. For by this time, other Indian tribes had moved into Indiana, too.

The Shell Mound Indians gathered clams for food.

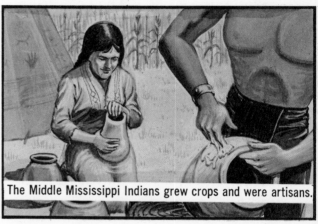
The Middle Mississippi Indians grew crops and were artisans.

The horse and buggy give way to the horseless carriage.

Today we fly in jet planes.

Like the prehistoric Indians, these Indians also made their tools and weapons out of stone and bone. But they had some made from wood as well.

The houses they lived in were round and were made by putting poles in the ground. The poles were forced together and tied at the top. Then branches from trees, usually willows, were woven through the poles. The huts were then covered with mats made from bark or animal skins.

These Indians had learned to make canoes, which they used both for fishing and for traveling. The canoes, made of birch bark, were so light that the Indians were able to carry them easily from one lake or river to another.

Like the early Indians, these Indians were also hunters and fishermen. While the men hunted and fished, the women took care of the gardens. They raised corn, beans, squash, pumpkins, peas and melons. Since the Indians liked to smoke, they also raised tobacco.

Although the Indians led a hard and dangerous life, they liked to have their fun and games, too. Dancing was an important part of their lives. They had dances for feast days, dances before the hunt and dances to honor the dead. They had many different dances.

Indian children were treated well. But they were expected to learn to do what their parents did. The girls had the same tasks as their mothers, such as gardening and cooking and caring for the younger children. The boys had to learn how to hunt and fish and fight.

In the beginning, when the white men first came, the Indians were willing to teach them how to live in this new land. They showed them how to raise the Indian foods. They traded furs gladly for the white men's goods.

But soon the white men began to come in greater numbers. The Indians were angry and afraid. The white men were not only taking away Indian lands, but they were driving away the animals. The Indians fought, hoping to keep their way of life and drive the white man back. But it was the Indians who were driven out of Indiana.

The unwritten history of the prehistoric Indian people began when the first Stone Age men crossed the land bridge from Asia to America. The written history of the historic Indians in Indiana began when Robert de La Salle stepped upon Indiana soil.

Chapter 4 . . . The White Man Comes to America

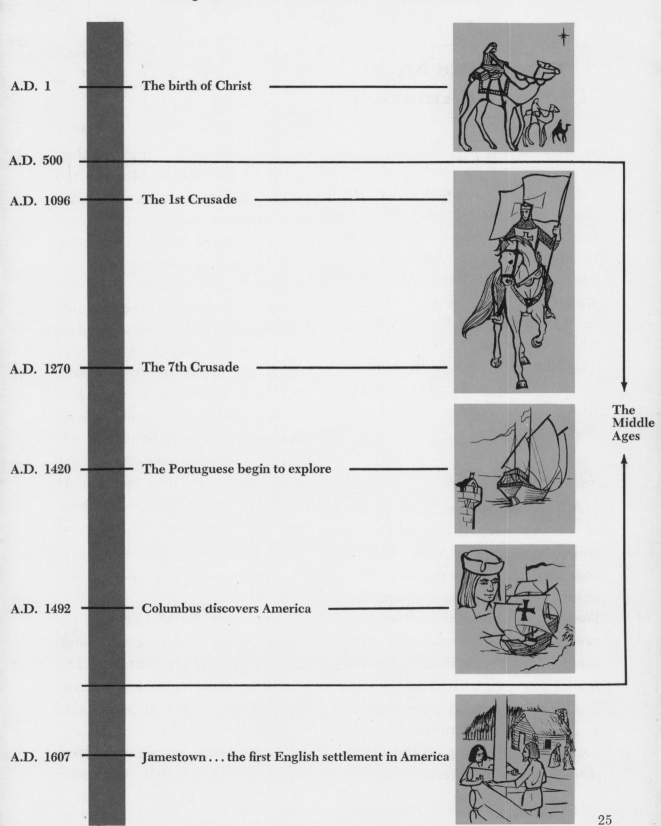

A.D. 1 — The birth of Christ

A.D. 500

A.D. 1096 — The 1st Crusade

A.D. 1270 — The 7th Crusade

The Middle Ages

A.D. 1420 — The Portuguese begin to explore

A.D. 1492 — Columbus discovers America

A.D. 1607 — Jamestown . . . the first English settlement in America

4

The White Man Comes to America

During the Middle Ages, nobles often fought one another.

Before the White Man Came

It must have seemed to the Indian that the white man came suddenly out of nowhere. But just as the history of the Indian began when the early Stone Man first crossed the land bridge from Asia to Alaska, so the history of the white man goes far back in time. The history of the white man in America really had its beginning in Europe long before America was discovered.

The Middle Ages

A thousand years ago, the people of Europe were living in a time called the "Middle Ages." During that time most of the people worked as farmers for large landowners. The landowners were called nobles. The nobles got their lands from their king. In return for their lands, the nobles promised to fight for the king whenever he needed their help.

The nobles also promised to protect the people living on their land. The people in turn were to farm the land and give part of the food they raised to the nobles. Most of the people had to do other work for their nobles, as well. They were not free to travel or move. They were little better than slaves.

The nobles lived in big houses or castles. From boyhood they learned to be fighting men. They obeyed no one but their king. If a king was strong, the nobles served him well. But if a king was weak, the nobles did what they liked. Under a weak king, nobles would fight one another. Bad nobles were cruel to the people, and acted like bandits. At times, powerful nobles would even fight with their kings.

The Christian Church

At the time the Middle Ages began, more and more people began to turn to the Christian church. The Christian church became strong, and was the center of learning in Europe.

Usually, only people who were taught by the church could read and write. There was little education outside the church. The church schools were mainly used to teach men who wanted to become priests.

People in the Middle Ages loved their religion and their church. This was true not only of the farmers and other working people, but of the kings and nobles as well.

Some of the people felt so strongly about their religion that they made special trips to Palestine, the Holy Land of the Bible. At this time the Holy Land was under the rule of people of a different religion. These people were called Moslems (mŏz′ləmz).

At first the Moslems allowed the Christians to come and pray in the Holy Land. But in the eleventh century, the Moslems did not want

the Christians in the Holy Land
any more. The Moslems began to
drive the Christians away. Soon it
was not safe for a Christian to enter
the Holy Land.

The Crusades

The people in western Europe
were angry and upset. They looked
on the Holy Land as an important
part of their religion. The men of
the church were angry, too. They
felt that the Holy Land was more
important to the Christians than it
was to the Moslems.

And so a new kind of war began.
It was called a "holy" war. The holy
wars were also known as the Crusades. The word Crusade comes
from the Latin word for "cross."
The men who fought in these wars
were called the Crusaders.

The first Crusade began A.D. 1095.
The seventh and last Crusade ended
about A.D. 1291. The knights fought
hard. Though the Crusaders won
many battles, they could not win
the Holy Land from the Moslems.

Important Changes After the Crusades

The Crusades had begun because the people wanted to free the Holy Land from the Moslems. The Crusades failed to do this. But other important happenings came about because of the Crusades.

Before the Crusades, the people of western Europe knew very little about the people in other lands. There were few big cities except in the country of Italy. And there was little trade between countries.

Now, because of the Crusades, people discovered many new things and new ideas. The Crusaders brought back products not known in western Europe. For example, the Crusaders brought back pepper, cinnamon, nutmeg and sugar. Before the Crusaders brought home these spices, the people had used little seasoning for their food except salt. Never had the people seen anything so beautiful as the jewelry, rugs, glass, fine cloth made of cotton and silk and other things from the East that the Crusaders showed them. Once they had seen all these things, the people of western Europe did not want to do without them. Because of this new trade, many new towns began to grow.

Crusaders brought back sugar, pepper, rugs, glassware and jewels.

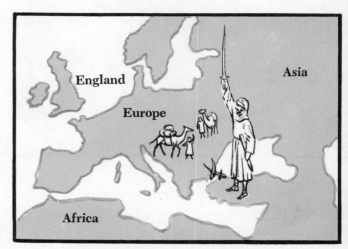

Moslems block trade routes to Asia

The Need for New Trade Routes Leads to The Discovery of America

The people of western Europe were very eager to trade with the East. But the Moslems were still in power. To trade with the eastern countries, traders had to find a new way to reach them. The traders could not go directly east, since they were blocked by the Moslems. They were forced to explore new routes.

A small country in western Europe, called Portugal, began to explore along the coast of Africa. The Portuguese had learned to build

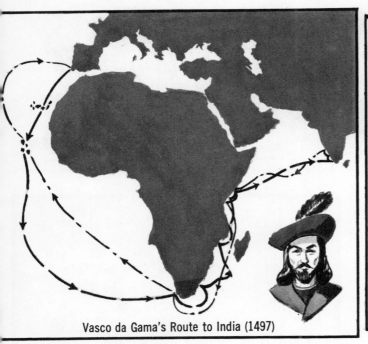

Vasco da Gama's Route to India (1497)

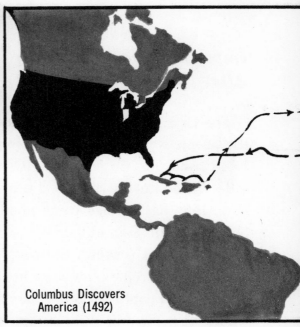

Columbus Discovers
America (1492)

better ships. They also used a new instrument called a compass. The compass helped them to find their way across the unknown seas.

A great Portuguese explorer, Vasco da Gama, was the first to sail around the coast of Africa. Soon other Portuguese ships sailed around the southern end of Africa and then on to India. The Portuguese set up trading centers there.

Because of this trade, the small country of Portugal became very rich. And Portugal controlled the routes around Africa to India.

Countries that wanted to trade with India had to look for other new routes. In 1492, the queen of Spain gave a man called Christopher Columbus three ships.

Christopher Columbus had an odd idea. Although most people thought the world was flat, he believed it was round. He said he could reach India by sailing west. What he found was not India but a new world. The New World was America.

The New World

At first the New World was a big disappointment. It was not India! The New World was not a busy trading center. It had no spices, or silks, or any of the other interesting and beautiful things that the Western world was looking for. And the only people in this New World were scattered tribes of Indians. But later, of course, the Spaniards were

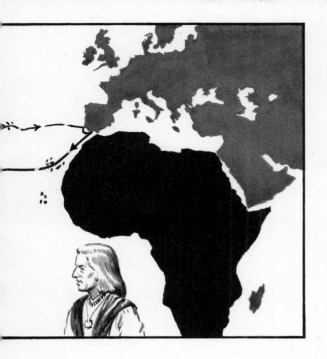

Why People of Europe Wanted to Come to America

People in western Europe came to America for many different reasons. Some men came because they hoped to become rich. They wanted to find gold or silver or pearls. They wanted to trade for fine furs. Many came because they wanted to become landowners in the New World.

Another important reason was the desire to worship God as they pleased. After the Middle Ages, new groups formed in the Christian church. Men with new ideas about religion were sometimes punished for their beliefs. Many people came to the English colonies in the search for religious freedom.

Others came because they did not like their government at home. Some wanted to escape punishment for fighting against their king. Many hoped to be free to think and speak as they pleased in the New World. There was more political freedom in the English colonies than in those of Spain or France.

And, of course, there were always men who looked for excitement and adventure. It was these men who explored the wild new country and opened up new territories for the settlers who would come after them.

to find gold, silver, tobacco and sugar cane in the new world.

Spanish explorers claimed the New World for Spain. Men with a spirit of adventure followed the explorers. Still other men wanted to come to America to preach Christianity to the Indians. These men were called missionaries. Soon there were colonies of white men living in America. In the beginning, these colonies were either Spanish or Portuguese. But other European countries wanted to settle in the New World. They sent out explorers, too. Soon they were fighting Spain and Portugal for a place in America. And before long, the Dutch, the French and the British also had colonies in America.

Chapter 5 . . . The French and British Fight for the New World

1630 to 1679 — The French explore the Great Lakes Area

1679 — Robert de La Salle enters Indiana

1681 — La Salle meets with Indian chiefs under the Council Oak

1682 — La Salle claims the Mississippi Valley for France

1717 to 1731 — The French build Forts Ouiatenon, Miamis and Vincennes in Indiana

1754 — The French and Indian War begins. The French and Indians fight the British and the American colonists.

1759 — The British capture Quebec, the capital of Canada

1763 — By the Treaty of 1763, the French give their Canadian lands and their lands east of the Mississippi River to the British. By the Proclamation of 1763, the British try to make friends with the Indians

1765 — The British pass the Stamp Tax

1770 — The Boston Massacre. British soldiers shoot American colonists in Boston, Mass.

5

The French and British Fight for the New World

English Colonial farmer

The Treasures of America

It was not long before different parts of America were being claimed for different countries in Europe. Most of the land in the south and southwest came under Spanish rule. Spanish soldiers of fortune came looking for gold and other treasures. Spanish priests came to preach Christianity to the Indians.

The French found treasure of another kind. They became fur traders and fishermen, as well as explorers. The area we know today as eastern Canada, and the land around the Great Lakes, became French territory. Before long, French explorers, along with missionaries and traders, followed the unknown rivers in the Mississippi Valley. These explorers claimed for France the land that was to be the Northwest Territory.

The British may have come looking for treasure, just as the Spanish and French did. But the treasure they found was the land itself. They began to farm the land and build permanent homes. Most of the peo-

ple who came from England started life in the New World as farmers.

The Spanish settled in the southwest. The British settled along the Atlantic Coast. And the French, at first, were interested only in the northern part of the new land. But as the French began to trade in furs with the Indians, they moved further into the center of the New World. They were more interested in trading than settling the land.

Robert de La Salle

In the year 1679, a young Frenchman named Robert de La Salle came to Indiana. He was the first white man to explore Indiana.

Robert de La Salle was a long way from his native land of France. Born into a rich and powerful family, La Salle received a fine education. His family expected him to become a priest. Instead, young Robert began to dream of this wild new country across the sea.

When he was twenty-three, La Salle could wait no longer. He sailed to New France, which was then the name for Canada. There he was given land, on which he set up a trading post. Indians came and traded with the young man, and found him eager to learn.

It was not enough for La Salle just to trade with the Indians. He learned their language. Soon the Indians began to tell the young man who asked so many questions about a great river. It was called the O-hē-yo, which in the Indian tongue meant "beautiful river." We call it the Ohio.

Soon La Salle sold his trading post. He wanted to see the land about which the Indians spoke. He may have discovered the great Ohio River which the Indians called beautiful.

Word of La Salle's discovery reached France. King Louis lost no time in claiming all of the Ohio Valley for France. Shortly after this, La Salle sailed home. The King made him a knight. He also asked La Salle to continue to explore the western part of New France and to build forts there.

The First White Man Enters Indiana

On a freezing day in December, 1679, La Salle and his men paddled up the icy waters of the St. Joseph River, near what is now South Bend, Indiana. La Salle was looking for a portage (pōr′tĭj) to take him to another river. A portage is a land path between rivers or lakes.

The Indians had told La Salle that he could reach the mouth of the Mississippi River by following several smaller rivers that flowed into it. Since La Salle's good friend and guide, White Beaver, had stayed behind to hunt deer, La Salle made up his mind to find the portage path by himself. He went out alone into the swampy land and soon was lost in the snow and darkness. He wandered around for three hours, firing his rifle and shouting. But no one from his camp heard him, and La Salle could not find his way back alone.

Suddenly, La Salle saw a small campfire through the trees. He crept quietly toward it. The camp fire and the bed of dry leaves close to it were deserted. La Salle was certain the camp belonged to an Indian, who must have been frightened away by La Salle's shouts and the gunfire.

La Salle shouted in all directions that he was going to spend the night in the camp. When he received no answer, he lay down and slept peacefully for the night.

LaSalle and his men enter Indiana on a freezing December day.

35

And so it was that the first white man in Indiana spent his first hours on Indiana soil lost in the wilderness. And he spent his first night on Indiana soil sleeping in the borrowed bed of an Indian.

The next morning La Salle had no trouble finding his own camp and men. White Beaver, who had returned, led La Salle and his men to the portage.

La Salle's Great Discovery

In 1682, La Salle did what no other white man before him had ever done. Other explorers had followed the Mississippi River part of the way.

Indian
tomahawk,
bow and
arrow

But La Salle followed the Mississippi River all the way down to where it emptied into the Gulf of Mexico. In the name of his king, he then claimed all the vast land around the Mississippi River for France.

In 1687, La Salle was killed by one of his own men while he was on still another exploration.

It was the daring of this great explorer that gave to France the Mississippi River Valley. It was Robert de La Salle who opened the way for French settlements in what was to become Indiana.

La Salle Unites the Indians

At the time La Salle was battling his way through the wilderness, a fierce group of eastern Indians was raiding Indian villages in Indiana. These Indians were the Iroquois (ĭr′ə-kwoi). British settlers called the Iroquois "The Five Nations," for five Indian tribes had joined together into one powerful group. The Iroquois were such fierce and savage fighters that even other Indian tribes feared them.

At one time several different tribes lived in Indiana. Among these were the Illinois Indians and the Miami Indians. But after their villages had been destroyed time and time again by the Iroquois, the other tribes fled from Indiana.

La Salle wanted to set up forts in different parts of the country, so French traders could come and go freely. But he knew he could not build forts unless he had some protection from the attacks of the Iroquois. He decided that he would have to get the Illinois and the Miami Indians, along with other tribes in Indiana, to fight together against the Iroquois.

In May, 1681, La Salle met with the chiefs of the different tribes. His faithful Indian friend, White

Beaver, helped him. There is a tree, now called the La Salle Council Oak, in South Bend. It was under this tree that La Salle met with the Indian chiefs, and asked them to join together for their own protection. The chiefs agreed. And soon the Indians returned to Indiana, building their villages all along the Wabash and the other rivers flowing through Indiana.

The French Forts

When the friendly Indians came back, the French were able at last to build forts for the traders. The traders lived at the forts. From the forts they went out to trade for furs with the Indians. In return for the furs, the traders gave the Indians such things as guns, knives, beads, blankets, needles and cloth.

The Indians did not mind having these forts built. There were not too many Frenchmen on their land. The Indians were not afraid then that the white men would spoil their hunting grounds. The French treated the Indians well and tried to keep them as friends.

At this time, three forts were built in Indiana. One was the Miami, which later became the city of Fort Wayne. The Miami fort was the first fur-trading fort in Indiana. Fort Ouiatenon (wē-ăt′ə-nōn) was built where the city of Lafayette now stands. The largest of the three forts was Fort Vincennes, which later became the city of Vincennes.

These forts were built not only to help the traders but to protect the valuable waterways from Canada to Louisiana.

For a while, life for the French

French soldier

settlers in the forts was good and free of care. They got along well with the Indians. Though the French did not fear the Indians, they would soon have reason to fear the British.

The French and British Go to War

The British settlers in the East were becoming restless. They wanted to see what lay behind the mountains. Many wanted land on which to build new farms and homes for their families. Traders, too, knew there was great wealth in furs beyond the mountains.

It was not long before the British traders began to take away some of the French fur trade. The Indians liked the French more, but they found that the British were willing to pay them twice as much for furs. So they began to trade with the British.

For a long time, the French and British had been enemies in Europe. Now they started to fight each other in America. This fight, which was called the French and Indian War, began in 1754.

The French wanted to keep the British settlers in the East. To do this, the French sent an army to build forts and roads in Western Pennsylvania. This land, the British said, belonged to them. They sent a young man, named George Washington, to tell the French to leave their territory. The French refused. It was then that the great fight for the New World began.

The British Win the War

In 1755, England sent one of its generals, Edward Braddock, to America with an army of British soldiers. George Washington served with this army, as did many Americans. Braddock decided to capture a strong French fort in what is now western Pennsylvania. Washington knew that the French and Indians were wise forest fighters. They did not fight in the open but hid behind rocks and trees.

Washington tried to tell the British that they could not fight in America as they did in Europe. But General Braddock would not listen to Washington. Braddock advanced with his troops as if he were on parade, with rolling drums and flying flags. The French and Indians prepared a trap and surprised the British. The general and many of his men were killed. Fortunately, Washington knew enough about Indian fighting to save what was left of the British army.

For several years, the war went badly for the British. But they found wiser generals and learned how to fight in the forest. Soon they began to push the French back.

In 1759, a battle took place that was to bring the war in America to an end. This was the great battle for Quebec, the most important city in Canada. Both the British and the French generals lost their lives in this battle.

The city of Quebec fell into the hands of the British. When this happened, the French and Indian War was over.

The British and the Indians

In 1763, the French signed a treaty of peace with the British. The French agreed to give to England all her lands in Canada and all the land east of the great Mississippi River. To Spain, which had helped England during the war, France gave up all the land west of the Mississippi.

After the treaty was signed, England kept soldiers in America to protect the newly-won lands. Now there were British soldiers in the French forts.

British soldie

The French settlers who remained behind in Indiana were still faithful to the King of France. And some of the Indian tribes did not like the new British rulers any more than the French did. British traders did not treat the Indians as well as the French had. The French had given the Indians many presents. When the British were not as generous, the Indians were insulted.

In spite of the fact that the war had been won by England, the French settlers and the Indians still hoped that the British could be driven away. Some of the French settlers let the Indians know they would be glad if the Indians would fight the British soldiers.

Pontiac's Revolt

An Indian war chief named Pontiac began to get Indian war parties together. He sent some of his men to attack Fort Miami and Fort Ouiatenon. Both these forts were forced to surrender. After the capture of these forts, Pontiac was in control of Indiana.

Pontiac then sent more war parties to attack other French forts that the British soldiers had taken over. Once again Pontiac's men were successful.

But in other forts, the British held out against Pontiac and his men. Finally, Pontiac's followers became tired. His plan to drive the British away failed.

The Proclamation of 1763

Pontiac's revolt made the British change their minds about how to rule their new lands. They decided to make new laws for the land they won from the French.

One of these laws was the "Proclamation of 1763." This Proclamation was meant to show the Indians that the British were friendly to them.

The Proclamation said that settlers in the east would not be allowed to move into Indian territory. The Indians were pleased, but the white settlers were angry.

The British Ask Americans to Pay Taxes

The French and Indian War had cost the British people a great deal of money. Pontiac's revolt showed that British soldiers were needed in America. The British government decided that the settlers in America should pay the costs of their own protection.

The Stamp Tax, 1765

One of the tax laws the British put through was the Stamp Act. This meant that the Americans would have to pay a tax on newspapers and legal papers. It was a most unpopular law in America.

Americans complained about being taxed when they did not have a part in making the tax laws. Many refused to pay the tax. Surprised at the anger of the settlers, the British government withdrew the Stamp Act in 1766.

The Americans Refuse to Pay Other Taxes

The next year, a new leader came to power in the British government. This man was Charles Townshend. He knew little about America or Americans. He thought Americans would be willing to pay taxes if they were small ones.

He got several laws passed which placed taxes on things that were brought from England to America. Paper, glass, lead and tea were some of the things taxed.

Townshend discovered that the Americans did not want to pay these new taxes either. Many people refused to buy the taxed goods. All through the colonies, people got

The Boston Massacre

up in town meetings and in the colonial legislatures to make speeches against the tax laws and the British.

The People of Boston Fight Back

The people of Boston, in Massachusetts, had been leaders in fighting the tax laws. They also objected to the British soldiers that were kept in the city. They called the red-coated British "lobsterbacks."

On March 5, 1770, a crowd gathered and began to shout and throw snowballs at a British soldier on duty at the Custom House where taxes were paid on goods brought

from England. Other soldiers came to help the man on duty.

In the excitement, a nervous soldier fired his gun. This was like a signal to the other soldiers who fired their guns. Some Americans were killed. Others were wounded. This fight between the British and the Americans was known as the Boston Massacre (măs′ə-kər).

Because the Americans were so angry, the British government withdrew all taxes except one. This was a three-penny tax on tea. A three-penny tax seems a small thing. But the tea tax was like a spark that started a fire. It was to lead to the American Revolution.

Chapter 6 .... Indiana and the American Revolution

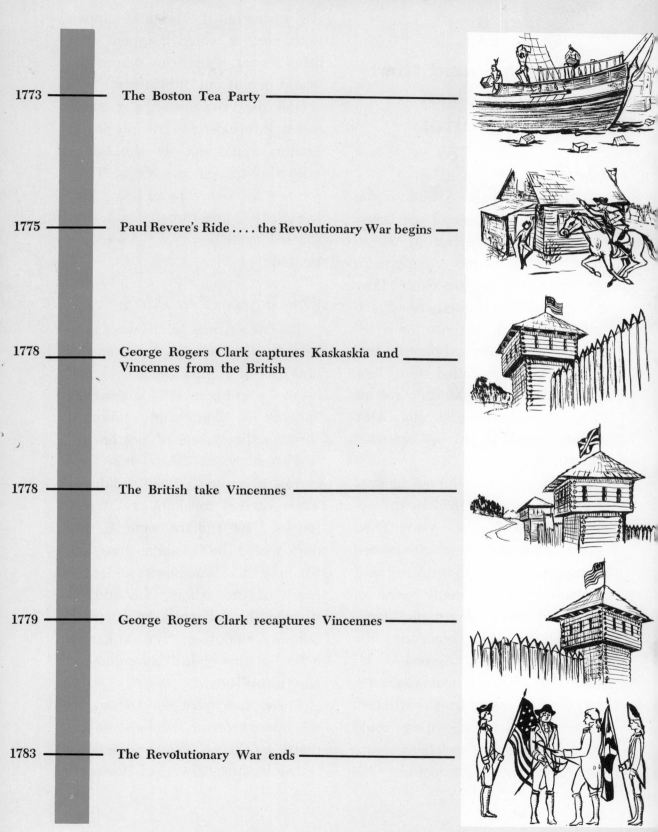

1773 ———— The Boston Tea Party —————

1775 ———— Paul Revere's Ride .... the Revolutionary War begins —

1778 ———— George Rogers Clark captures Kaskaskia and ————
Vincennes from the British

1778 ———— The British take Vincennes —————

1779 ———— George Rogers Clark recaptures Vincennes ————

1783 ———— The Revolutionary War ends —————

6

Indiana and the American Revolution

The Tea Tax

After the Boston Massacre the British gave up most of the taxes. But they kept the tax on tea to show that they had the right to tax the American colonists. Many Americans refused to buy tea. Some colonists brought tea into the country secretly without paying the tax. These men were called smugglers. The British used small sailing ships to try to catch the smugglers. One of the British ships was captured and burned.

Although they spoke out against the tea tax, most Americans accepted the tax for three years. Then something happened which angered them again. A British company that shipped goods to many parts of the world was having money troubles. To help this company, the British government agreed to let them ship tea to the colonies without paying taxes to the British. This meant that the company could sell tea in America for less than any American merchant could. The Americans felt if this could happen with tea, it could happen with other goods. American merchants would be put out of business.

One day three company ships sailed into Boston. The people of Boston would not let the sailors take the tea off the ships. They wanted the tea ships to leave. But the British government said that the tea must be unloaded and the tax paid.

The Boston Tea Party

The Americans felt it was time to show their anger in action and not just in words. On a cold December evening in 1773, a group of Indians in war paint marched through the streets of Boston. All had feathers in their hair and blankets around their shoulders. They carried muskets and tomahawks. The Indians went to the dock where the tea ships were tied. Shaking their tomahawks under the noses of the sailors, the Indians warned the sailors to keep out of the way. Shouting, "Boston harbor a tea-pot this night!" they dumped the tea overboard.

These men were not Indians at all, but white men dressed as Indians. In the war party were some of the leading citizens of Boston.

The British government could not let the colonists go unpunished. In anger they passed a law closing the port of Boston until all the tea was paid for. The colony of Massachusetts also lost many of its rights of self-government. And still another British law allowed British soldiers to live in the homes of the people. Think how you would feel if a soldier from another country forced his way in and lived in your house!

The other colonies did not like what was happening to Massachusetts and Boston. Now there was open talk against the British government. The important men in the colonies got together to decide what should be done. This meeting, which was held in Philadelphia, was called the First Continental Congress. As a result of this meeting, gunpowder and muskets were collected. Companies of Americans began to drill in the villages.

The Fight for Liberty Begins

More British soldiers were sent to America. The British sent some soldiers from Boston to seize the guns and gunpowder stored in the little town of Concord.

On the night of April 18, 1775, two Americans made a famous ride. They were Paul Revere and William Dawes. On that night they rode across the countryside to warn the Americans that British soldiers were coming.

American farmers gathered at Lexington on the road from Boston. There, when the British troops came, the first battle of the American Revolution took place. Before the fight for liberty ended, many men would lay down their lives to bring freedom to their land. But when the American Revolution was over, there would be a new country on the map of the world—the United States of America.

George Rogers Clark

A map of the country at the beginning of the American Revolution shows that Indiana was still an unmarked part of the continent. At that time, it was just a part of the old Northwest. Much of the Revolution was fought near the eastern seacoast. But one important part of the Revolution took place in what is now the Midwest. And land that would later be part of Indiana was important.

The story of the Revolution in the Midwest is really the story of a man named George Rogers Clark.

A French musket and powder horn used by American soldiers

Young Clark surveying in the wilderness

George Rogers Clark was born in Virginia in 1752 where his father owned a large plantation. Since the Clarks lived near the Jefferson plantation, George Rogers Clark and Thomas Jefferson became friends.

As a boy, George Rogers Clark was sent to some good schools. But he always liked the woods better. He became a fine outdoorsman and hunter.

When Clark grew up, he was a big man, well over six feet tall. This red-headed young man was a natural leader. At the age of nineteen, he went over the mountains to Pittsburgh. He became a surveyor on the upper Ohio River. While surveying along the Ohio, George Rogers Clark also claimed some valuable land there.

Pioneer Scout

Clark took naturally to the wilderness. He loved it, even though its ways were often hard. He wrote to his brother: "A richer and more beautiful country than this . . . has never been seen in America." Clark came to know and like the pioneers who were settling the land. He also began to learn much about the Indians he met, although they were not always friendly.

While Clark was surveying along the Ohio, an Indian uprising took place. Clark became a special scout for the British and was made a captain in the army by the British governor. The Indian uprising was put down within a few months. Clark then decided to move on to Kentucky. At this time, the Americans were not yet at war with the British.

In 1775, many pioneers were moving into the new wilderness of Kentucky. Among these was Daniel Boone, who made a famous trail called the "Wilderness Road." Boone's trail led from Virginia through the Cumberland Gap into Kentucky. At the end of this trail, Boone began the settlement of Boonesborough.

George Rogers Clark, too, was among these first great pioneers who entered the "Dark and Bloody Ground." This was the name given to Kentucky because of the many bloody Indian battles fought there. Clark surveyed for the settlers, and also claimed land for himself. He liked this wild Kentucky country.

The Indian Attacks

Indians living north of the Ohio River began to attack the new settlements. The Indians had good reason to go on the warpath. They had already lost much land to white settlers. They wondered how long it would be before these settlers crossed the Ohio River and began to settle northward.

The British gave the Indians guns. They wanted the Indians to destroy the new settlements in Kentucky. The British had no wish to see the Americans settling in the west. And so they did all they could to help the Indians in their war against the settlers.

Clark's Plan for Kentucky

George Rogers Clark soon became a leader among the Kentucky settlers. He was only 23 years old at this time. But this tall, strong redhead had seen as much of the new territory as any man. And he also had had experience in fighting Indians.

He had a plan for the Kentucky settlements. He wanted Kentucky to be made a county belonging to Virginia. Many of the settlers had come from Virginia. If Clark could get Virginia to claim Kentucky, then Virginia would have to help Kentucky in its fight against the Indians. Clark knew his plan would help not only Kentucky, but also the American colonies who were

AN INDIAN
TOMAHAWK

now waging war with the British.

Clark went to Virginia to explain his plan and to ask for money and supplies for an army. He knew that the Indians were being helped by British troops at Vincennes and Kaskaskia. If George Rogers Clark could capture these British strongholds, he would help the Revolution and also help the Kentucky settlers at the same time. When Clark came back from Virginia, he sent scouting parties to see how strong the British were at Kaskaskia and Vincennes. He soon learned that there were few British soldiers at either one of the places.

Like all the other colonies, Virginia had to supply men and money for the regular army. That took almost all she could afford. But Virginia finally gave Clark a small amount of money to pay for enough men to carry out the attack he had planned.

George Rogers Clark Captures Two Forts

Although it was very hard to do, Clark finally got together a small force of about 170 men. He trained them on an island in the Ohio River, near what is now Jeffersonville, Indiana.

He began his surprise attack on Kaskaskia on June 24, 1778. On his way to Kaskaskia, Clark met some hunters. The hunters felt sure the British did not know Clark was coming. Clark decided to march overland to Kaskaskia. It was over a hundred miles, but Clark marched his men hard and fast. They arrived in six days.

Clark slipped into the town of Kaskaskia in the middle of the night. He captured it without firing a shot. The British gave up almost at once.

Then Clark learned something new. The British had already left Fort Sackville at Vincennes. The old fort was deserted. All Clark had to do was send someone to take it over. This he did right away. So within a day's time, Clark had taken over both of the British forts he had set out to capture.

Now Clark set about making peace with the Indians. He called a council of chiefs and spoke to them boldly. He said, "I am a man and a warrior. I carry war in my right hand and peace in my left hand. I was sent by the council fire of the Big Knives [the Indian name for the Americans] to take control of all the towns the British possess in this country, and to remain here watching the conduct of the redmen."

PENNSYLVANIA
RIFLE

49

Clark holds aloft belts of war and peace.

Then Clark held up two belts. He said to the chiefs: "Here is a bloody belt and a white one. Take whichever you please."

The Indians liked the bold and honest speech Clark made. They chose the white belt of peace and said they had been fooled by the lies of the British.

The British Arrive At Vincennes

While Clark was dealing with the Indians, the British were themselves planning an attack. The British leader, Henry Hamilton, got word of Clark's victories. Hamilton had been in charge of the Indian attacks on Kentucky. When he heard what Clark had done, he decided to attack at once.

Hamilton arrived at Vincennes with his army in the middle of December. Clark had left only two men at Old Fort Sackville. They could not fight an army of 600 men. They had to surrender.

Hamilton learned that many of the rivers in Southern Indiana and Illinois were running over their banks. He knew that the lowlands were flooded. Because of the bad weather, and the fact that his soldiers were tired from their long trip across Indiana, Hamilton decided to stay at Vincennes. He would strengthen Fort Sackville while he waited for better weather in the spring.

Late in January, a fur trader arrived at Kaskaskia. His name was Francis Vigo. He went to see George Rogers Clark, to tell him what had happened at Vincennes. Vigo also knew Hamilton planned to march against Kaskaskia in the spring.

The Great Decision

If George Rogers Clark had given up at this point, no one would have blamed him. He had no money left to buy supplies, and some of his men had already gone home. What could one man do?

It was the middle of winter. Could he get to Vincennes in the bitter cold? Could he get men to go with him? Could he raise more money? He told Francis Vigo what he wanted to do, and Vigo agreed to lend him money. Another trader also let Clark have supplies for which Clark could pay him later.

George Rogers Clark made his decision. He would move against the British at Vincennes in the dead of winter. It must be now or never. By spring, the British would be too strong. If he and his men were to have any chance at all, they would have to take the British by surprise.

On the morning of February 5, 1779, Clark's small army of about 125 men set out to march across Illinois to Vincennes. Clark had sent a large boat down the Mississippi the day before. On board were about fifty of Clark's men. The boat was to travel down to the Ohio river and then follow the Wabash River up to Vincennes. The boat also carried a lot of Clark's supplies and ammunition.

Clark planned to march straight across Illinois. He did not want to follow any of the usual trails. He thought he could save time by cutting straight across. So the almost impossible march began.

The Terrible March

Clark soon learned that heavy rains had softened the ground. Walking was very difficult. In many places, too, streams had overrun their banks. The hunters could not find game, and Clark's soldiers were hungry. Soon the men wanted to give up. Clark laughed and told jokes to keep them going. Whenever he wanted his men to march, he marched ahead of them. When they crossed dangerously-swollen rivers, Clark went into the cold water first.

Once Clark put a little French drummer boy on the shoulders of a big soldier and told him to beat his drum. He sang marching songs and kept singing until the voices of his men rang out in song too.

They were getting near the British fort when their food ran out. Without food, the men had no strength to go on. But somehow Clark kept his men going. He was desperate. He had come so far and gone through so much. He *had* to reach Vincennes. This would be his only chance to take the British by surprise.

Then came the worst blow of all. Clark's boat, with the supplies, failed to show up. Once again, Clark had to make an important decision. Should he go on without supplies and ammunition? Clark's decision was that he could not turn back. He knew his tired men could not march back across the swampy country without food.

Clark borrowed some hunters' boats and got his men across the river. The Wabash had overflowed its banks. The land on the other side was swampy. Great stretches of water lay between them and the fort at Vincennes.

Clark Captures Vincennes

The men wanted to give up. They had not eaten for two days. Now a sea of water and mud lay ahead of them. But Clark was not going to see his plan fail now. He was too close to his goal. He gave a war whoop and jumped into the water and mud. The men watched their redheaded leader with surprise. Then they slowly followed him into the chest-deep water.

The next morning, February 23, Clark's army was just a few miles below the fort. The men were now so tired they could hardly walk. But Clark talked to them about their bravery and about all they had overcome. He said that they only had to go a few more miles.

So it was that Clark led his little band on. A weaker leader would have failed. His men would have deserted him. Only a great leader could have brought his soldiers through this almost impossible march alive and ready to fight. Clark was such a leader.

Clark and his band finally found dry ground about two miles from the town and fort. Now, if they could capture Vincennes, they would have food and warmth. Clark just had to capture the town.

Clark sent a message to the people of the town, telling them that a large army was nearby. He said that he wished those who were friendly with the British to go to the fort. Anyone friendly to the American cause should stay in his house. Then Clark marched his men behind a high hill. He had several men carry tall flags. The people in the town could see only the flags. They thought there must be many troops with Clark.

The Attack On Fort Sackville

At dark, Clark marched into Vincennes. The town was his. And when he began to fire on Fort Sackville, the British were taken completely by surprise. No one from the town had gone to join the British troops in the fort.

Hamilton, the British commander, could not believe what was happening. How could an army have crossed Illinois? How could they have come across that sea of freezing water and mud? And yet they had. They were attacking.

Hamilton fought back. But the Kentucky sharpshooters were better shots than the British. Each time a British soldier peeked out from a crack, a lead ball would come through it. The good shooting, and the complete surprise of the attack, were too much for the British. On the morning of February 25, 1779, Hamilton surrendered his entire force. Clark had won Vincennes and Fort Sackville.

The New Lands for America

All that Clark had done, he had done in the name of Virginia. But he had done it for the American government as well. His victories were among the most important in all of the Revolutionary War. His winning of Kaskaskia and Vincennes meant that the American government would be able to add all of the old Northwest to their other territory. Of course, Virginia had a private claim on the land, too.

Dividing the land had to wait, however. There was still a war to win. It would take two more years for the Americans to silence the British guns. But the Northwest would finally be divided. And the area that would later become Indiana was an important part of that territory.

Kentucky sharpshooter

Chapter 7 . . . Indian Wars and Early Settlements

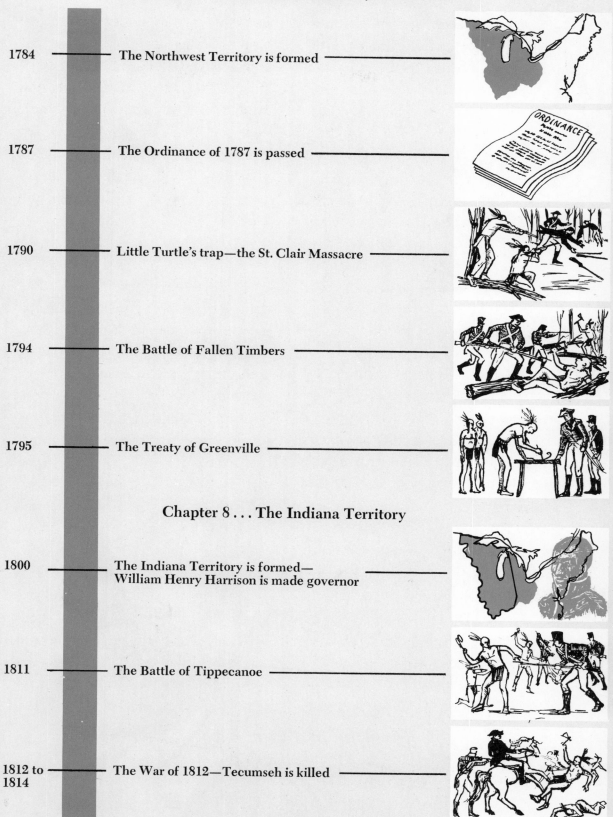

1784 — The Northwest Territory is formed

1787 — The Ordinance of 1787 is passed

1790 — Little Turtle's trap—the St. Clair Massacre

1794 — The Battle of Fallen Timbers

1795 — The Treaty of Greenville

Chapter 8 . . . The Indiana Territory

1800 — The Indiana Territory is formed—
William Henry Harrison is made governor

1811 — The Battle of Tippecanoe

1812 to 1814 — The War of 1812—Tecumseh is killed

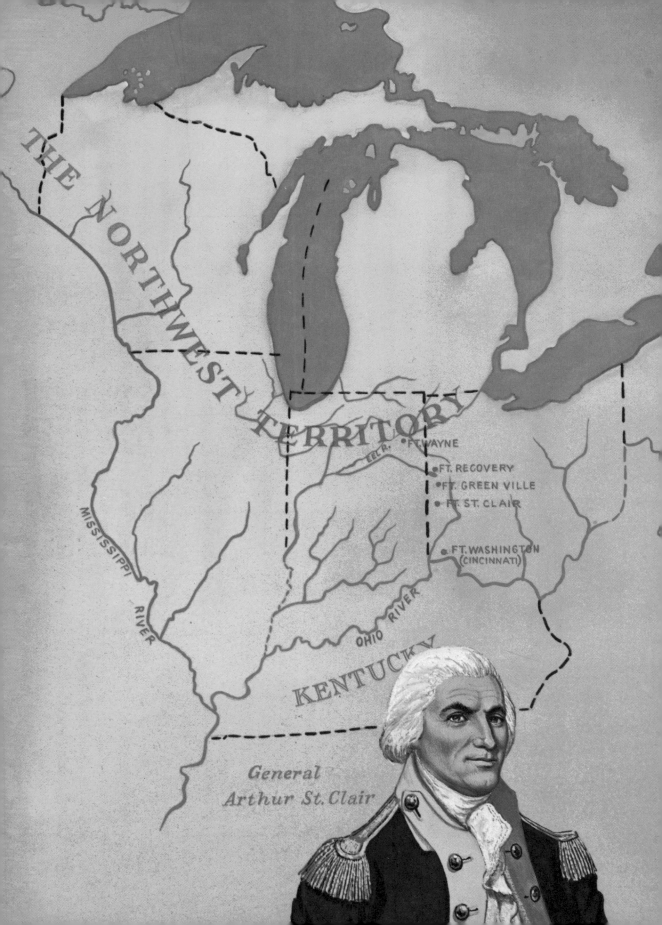

THE NORTHWEST TERRITORY

MISSISSIPPI RIVER

• FT. WAYNE
EEL R.
• FT. RECOVERY
• FT. GREEN VILLE
• FT. ST. CLAIR

• FT. WASHINGTON
(CINCINNATI)

OHIO RIVER

KENTUCKY

General
Arthur St. Clair

*Chief
Little Turtle*

*General
Anthony Wayne*

7

Indian Wars and Early Settlements

After the American Revolution

The Treaty of 1783 ended the American Revolution. But freedom from the British did not bring peace to the great land in the Midwest.

For thousands of Indians and some British soldiers still lived there.

When the Treaty of 1783 was written, the Indians were angry. In this Treaty, the British had agreed to give much Indian land in the north to the United States. But the Treaty had not even mentioned the Indians, who had not agreed to give their lands to anyone. The Indians feared the American settlers would take their lands.

The Indians Make War Plans

Chief Little Turtle, of the powerful Miami tribe, called a grand war meeting, or council. Most of the warriors at the council were Miamis. Although the Indians had often raided before their war council took place, they now planned even more raids north of the Ohio River. And they decided to make war on Kentucky.

George Rogers Clark Returns

George Rogers Clark heard about the Indian plan. He felt someone had to stop the Indian attacks. In the summer of 1786 he brought over 1,000 soldiers from Kentucky.

Clark and his men marched from Kentucky to Vincennes, where they waited for their food to arrive. But the food, which had been sent down the Ohio River and up the Wabash to Vincennes, had spoiled along the way.

Clark's army was hungry, poor and unhappy. There was no money to buy more food. The American Revolution had cost Virginia and the other states a lot of money. And Virginia could not spare any more money to help the brave general buy food for his army.

But George Rogers Clark had never been the kind of man to give up easily, even though many of his soldiers deserted him. He arranged a meeting with a few of the leading Indian chiefs. Because many of the chiefs admired Clark, he was able to talk them out of their plans for war on the Americans.

The Northwest Territory Is Formed

In the meantime, the United States had been deciding just what to do with the western land it had won from the British. Some of the new states said that the western lands belonged to them. Virginia felt that it had the first right to the western lands because it had done the most to fight the British there. After all, George Rogers Clark was a Virginian.

But then the state of Virginia decided that this was no time to be selfish. In March of 1784 it gave the land that it claimed northwest of the Ohio River to the United States. This was the land that later became Indiana, Illinois, Ohio, Michigan, Wisconsin and a part of Minnesota. The United States named its new land the Northwest Territory.

Almost the first thing Congress did for the Northwest Territory was to pass a set of laws called the Land

Ordinance of 1785. These laws made it possible for settlers to buy land in the Northwest Territory.

Before a settler could buy a piece of land, the United States had to buy the land from the Indians. Then the land had to be surveyed, or marked out.

The men who surveyed the land marked it out in squares with six-mile sides. Such a square was called a township. A township was then divided into thirty-six sections. Each section was one mile square and contained 640 acres. The United States would sell no less than one section at no less than one dollar per acre.

One section of each township was to be set aside for schools. For then, as now, the government of the United States believed that Americans needed good educations to become good citizens.

The High Price of Land

By charging at least $640 for a piece of land, Congress thought it could get back some of the money that was spent in fighting the Revolutionary War. But very few settlers had $640, which was a lot of money in those days. And 640 acres was more land than a settler could farm by himself. Only a company had enough money to buy so much land.

It was not surprising, then, that one of the first large land sales in the Northwest Territory was made to a company and not to a settler. The Ohio Company arranged to buy several million acres in southeastern Ohio. The company planned to sell small pieces of the land to settlers. In that way, the company could make a profit on each sale.

The Ordinance of 1787

More and more settlers bought land from companies. The Congress of the United States soon realized that the settlers had to have some laws to govern themselves.

Congress drew up a set of laws for the Northwest Territory. All of these laws together are called the Ordinance of 1787.

The Ordinance said the Northwest Territory would have a governor, three judges and a secretary.

At first, the governor, the judges and the secretary were not elected by the settlers, but were chosen by the Congress of the United States.

One of the most important laws in the Ordinance gave the settlers freedom of religion. This law allowed a settler to worship in any kind of church he pleased.

It was also against the law to

have slaves. No man could own, buy or sell another man.

The Ordinance also said that any area of the Northwest Territory could become a state if enough people lived in it.

More Indian Problems

The Ordinance of 1787 meant nothing to the Indians in the Northwest Territory. As more and more settlers came to the Northwest Territory and Kentucky, the Indians grew angrier and angrier.

The Indians decided to carry out the war plans they had made at Little Turtle's war council the year before. They began to raid the settlers again. In the first seven years after the Revolutionary War, Indians killed over 1,500 settlers in Kentucky. Abraham Lincoln's grandfather was killed in one of these Kentucky raids.

President George Washington worried about the Indian raids. He wrote a letter to Governor St. Clair, ordering him to ask the Indians whether they wanted peace or war. The governor warned the Indians that if they wanted peace, they would have to stop their raids on the settlers. The Indians refused to stop their raids unless the settlers left the Territory.

Chief Little Turtle's Trap

Governor St. Clair knew that the only way to stop the Indians was to fight them. So he sent General Josiah Harmar and a small army of American soldiers to stop the Indians raids. General Harmar and his soldiers marched north to an Indian village, where Fort Wayne now stands.

Chief Little Turtle was a clever warrior. When he heard that the soldiers were coming, he told the Miamis to leave their village. When the soldiers reached the Indian village, the Indians were not there. The Americans knocked down the empty Miami huts and burned the corn the Indians had left.

Four days later, General Harmar sent some soldiers along a trail that led to some Miami villages on the Eel River. One of the Indian camps looked empty. The soldiers dropped their rifles and began to gather up supplies lying around the camp. Suddenly, horrible yells burst from the trees around the camp.

The yells were Miami war whoops. Little Turtle had set a neat trap. He had caught the soldiers with their rifles on the ground. Many soldiers ran away, and those who stayed to fight were killed.

The St. Clair Massacre

In the meantime, Little Turtle had brought together a large army of warriors. There were braves from many Indian tribes.

Governor St. Clair himself had decided to lead a new army to put down the Indians. But his soldiers were slow and poorly trained. When the Governor's army reached a place near what is now Portland, Indiana, it camped for the night. And then, just before dawn, Little Turtle's army struck.

Whooping and screaming, the Indian warriors attacked the sleeping soldiers. Although Governor St. Clair escaped, almost half his soldiers were killed. It was the worst beating the American army had ever taken.

William Wells

One of Chief Little Turtle's best warriors in the St. Clair Massacre was a fierce fighter named Blacksnake. But Blacksnake was not an Indian. He was a white man whose real name was William Wells. When he was a boy, William had been captured by Little Turtle during one of his raids on Kentucky settlers.

William Wells was only eleven when he was captured. He was a strong, redheaded boy who could

read and write. Little Turtle and his Miamis named him Apekonit (ă-pē-kŏn'ət), which means wild potato in the Miami language. He was so quick and strong that the Miamis knew he would become a great warrior. As Wild Potato grew older, he was taken into the Miami tribe as a real Indian. Wild Potato was glad, for he had learned to love Little Turtle and the Miami people.

"Mad" Anthony Wayne and President George Washington

Wild Potato became such a fine warrior that the Miamis gave him a new name, Blacksnake. Blacksnake had known that Governor St. Clair's army could not fight without its officers or cannons. So when they attacked the camp just before dawn, Blacksnake's warriors fired first at the officers and the soldiers who manned the cannon.

The Indian marksmen did not miss their targets, and that was one reason so many of Governor St. Clair's soldiers were killed. The American soldiers had few officers alive to lead them, and no cannon to protect them.

George Washington Finds a New General

When President Washington heard the news of the St. Clair Massacre, he was very angry. He looked for and found a new general.

The man President Washington chose to fight the Indians was very brave and clever. In the Revolutionary War he had beaten the British in battles that other soldiers said he could not win. His name was "Mad Anthony" Wayne.

For two years General Wayne worked to build an army that could fight a wilderness war. And in two years, he had an army to be proud of. Every man had a good rifle. Some of Anthony Wayne's sharpshooters could knock a squirrel out of a tree at 100 yards.

While "Mad Anthony" Wayne had been training his army, President Washington had sent many peace offers to the Indians. But the Indians sent back the scalps of the messengers as their answer. The President knew then that the time had come to strike back. He ordered General Wayne's army to go after the Indians, who soon found out about the army moving against them.

The Battle of Fallen Timbers

Word of "Mad Anthony" Wayne had spread among the Indians. He became known as "the man who never sleeps." For General Wayne and his army were always on guard, and they marched north so fast that they never seemed to sleep.

"Mad Anthony" knew that the warriors of ten Indian tribes were waiting to do battle. He sent them one last peace offer.

When Little Turtle heard the peace offer, he tried to talk the Indians out of fighting the battle he thought they would lose. But the Indians called Little Turtle a coward and said that his blood had

turned to water. And they made Bluejacket, a Shawnee Indian, their new chief. Then the Indians sent word to Anthony Wayne that they would answer his peace offer in ten days.

"Mad Anthony" Wayne knew that in ten days the Indians could get help from the British, who were nearby in a strong fort named Fort Miamis. So General Wayne decided to fight the Indians at once.

The Indians were waiting at Fallen Timbers, a place where a tornado had torn down many big trees. The fallen trees gave the Indians good places to hide.

"Mad Anthony" Wayne and his army moved ahead quickly. With his riflemen guarded on each side by galloping horsemen, he charged straight into the place of fallen timbers.

The surprised Indians barely had time to shoot more than once. With the long, sharp bayonets attached to their rifles, General Wayne's army chased the Indians out from behind the fallen trees. Many Indians were killed on the spot.

In one hour, the American army had the remaining Indians running toward Fort Miamis. As the Indians drew near the fort, the British shut

the fort gates in the faces of their Indian "friends." And that was a lucky thing for the British, because General Wayne was ready to destroy the British fort if it gave shelter to the Indians.

After the Battle of Fallen Timbers, the Indians no longer trusted the British. For when the Indians had really needed help, the British had failed them.

The beaten Indians crept back to their villages. They knew that Little Turtle had been right when he tried to talk them out of their battle with the Americans. Once again they made Little Turtle their chief.

The Treaty of Greenville

Now, when General Wayne sent them peace messages, the Indians listened more carefully. Little Turtle called together many chiefs. They all traveled to Fort Greenville, to smoke the peace pipe with General Wayne.

Anthony Wayne was a great Indian fighter, but he did not hate the Indians. So he spoke to them as one Indian chief would speak to another. He told them what lands the United States wanted to buy and what lands the Indians could keep.

Two months later, on August 3, 1795, Anthony Wayne and the Indians signed the Treaty of Greenville. It was an agreement as to which lands now belonged to the Indians and which lands belonged to the United States.

After he had signed the treaty with his mark, Little Turtle said, "I have been the last to sign it, and I will be the last to break it."

Now, more of the great new land would be safer for settlers and their families.

Soon after the treaty, more settlers than ever before to come to the Northwest Territory. And that was the most important result of the Treaty of Greenville.

The Northwest Territory Government Changes

Before 1798, the settlers had to use the laws made by the governor and the judges. But in 1798, Governor St. Clair announced some new laws for the Northwest Territory.

One new law allowed settlers to vote, if they owned enough land.

Another new law allowed settlers, if they owned enough land, to elect a man who would speak for them in the Congress of the United States. Such a man was called a delegate to Congress. As their first delegate to Congress, the settlers elected William Henry Harrison. He was a brave and intelligent man who had fought beside Anthony Wayne.

When William Henry Harrison was elected, a settler had to have at least fifty acres of land to vote. But Harrison did not think this was fair to the poorer settlers, and he did something about it. He decided settlers could buy land more easily, by paying for it a little at a time.

Soon the name of William Henry Harrison was well known throughout the country. In time, he would be President of the United States. But many exciting things were still ahead for this fine soldier before he stepped into the White House.

The first capital at Vincennes,
1800-1813

Governor
William Henry Harrison

THE INDIANA TERRITORY IN 1800

8

The Indiana Territory

The First Governor

In 1800, Congress split the Northwest Territory into two parts. The land west of what is now the state of Ohio became the Indiana Territory. President Adams made William Henry Harrison the first governor of the new Indiana Territory.

Buying Land From the Indians

Governor Harrison knew that he had to buy more land from the Indians, for more new settlers were coming than ever before. And the Indians still owned most of the land in the Indiana Territory.

Between 1801 and 1809, Governor Harrison made eight land treaties with the Indians. By these treaties, the United States government bought millions of acres of land in the Indiana Territory.

William Henry Harrison and Tecumseh disagree over land treaties.

Tecumseh (tĭ-kŭm′sə)

One of the Indian leaders, Tecumseh, did not want to sell Indian land to the Americans. For years, Tecumseh had talked to the Indian tribes in Indiana. He had tried to bring the Indian tribes together, so they could agree whether or not to sell their lands to the United States. Tecumseh knew that if the different tribes kept making separate treaties with Governor Harrison, the Indians would soon have no land left to themselves.

The Battle of Tippecanoe

Governor Harrison had just finished his last and greatest land treaty with the Indians at Fort Wayne. The north boundary of the land gained by this treaty is called the "Ten o' Clock Line" because it ran in the same direction as a shadow made by the sun at ten o'clock in the morning. After the treaty was finished, Governor Harrison returned to the town of Vincennes, which was the capital of the Indiana Territory.

Tecumseh soon came to Vincennes and told Governor Harrison that the Indian chiefs at Fort Wayne had no right to sell the Indian land. He said that he would kill the Indian chiefs who had sold land to the United States. Tecumseh also said he and his followers would shoot any settler who tried to live on the Indian land.

Governor Harrison tried to reason with Tecumseh, but the Indian would not change his mind. It was then that Governor Harrison knew he would have to show Tecumseh who was stronger.

With 1,000 soldiers, Governor Harrison marched up the east bank of the Wabash River to a place very near the Indian village of Prophetstown, about six miles north of what is now Lafayette, Indiana. A few Indians came from the town and told the governor that the Indians wanted to have a council with him the next morning. Governor Harrison ordered the camp guards to be watchful during the night and to keep their rifles loaded.

Just before dawn, the Indians made a surprise attack. They killed sixty of Governor Harrison's soldiers, but the Americans finally beat off the Indian attack. Then they entered Prophetstown and burned it to the ground.

The War of 1812

While Governor Harrison was having his troubles with the Indians, the United States was having more troubles with the British. There was some proof that the Indians had been working for the British. That angered the United States. The British had angered the United States even more by taking sailors off American ships and making them work on British ships.

For these reasons, the United States and Great Britain went to war again. Because the war began in 1812, it is called the War of 1812. Soon after the war started, the British and the Indians captured two American forts, Fort Detroit and Fort Dearborn.

The End of the War

General Harrison fought bravely as commander of an American army west of the Indiana Territory. He and his soldiers beat a British army and an Indian army led by Tecumseh. In another battle, Tecumseh was killed. Tecumseh had been a brave Indian. He had fought for what he thought was right.

Not long after Tecumseh was killed, the War of 1812 ended. American soldiers had pushed the British back into Canada. And the British had learned to respect the American navy on the oceans and on the Great Lakes. A peace treaty was signed on Christmas Eve, 1814.

After the war, the Indiana Territory had fewer problems with the Indians. More settlers came to the Indiana Territory than ever before. These settlers were hard-working men and women who wanted their land to be a state.

Chapter 9 . . . The Coming of the Pioneers

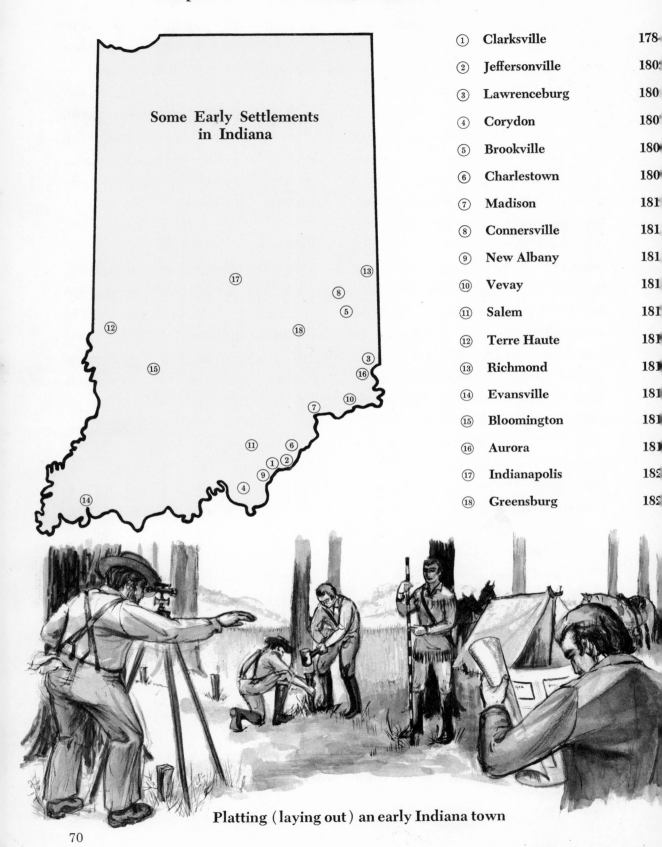

Some Early Settlements in Indiana

①	Clarksville	178.
②	Jeffersonville	180.
③	Lawrenceburg	180
④	Corydon	180.
⑤	Brookville	180
⑥	Charlestown	180
⑦	Madison	181
⑧	Connersville	181
⑨	New Albany	181
⑩	Vevay	181
⑪	Salem	181
⑫	Terre Haute	181
⑬	Richmond	181
⑭	Evansville	181
⑮	Bloomington	181
⑯	Aurora	181
⑰	Indianapolis	182
⑱	Greensburg	182

Platting (laying out) an early Indiana town

9

The Coming of the Pioneers

Who They Were

The earliest American settlers to live in what is now Indiana were some of George Rogers Clark's soldiers. To thank the soldiers for their help in the Revolutionary War, Virginia had given them a large piece of land in southern Indiana. There, overlooking the beautiful Ohio River, the town of Clarksville was born in 1784. In Clarksville, General George Rogers Clark built his home.

A few other early Indiana settlers lived in Vincennes. The Piankashaw (pĭ-ăng′kə-shô) Indians, who were friendly with the French settlers in Vincennes, had given the French a large piece of land there, The French were generous to new settlers, and they gave each new settler 400 acres of this land. By 1787, there were more than 100 American settlers and their families living in or near Vincennes.

Still other early Indiana settlers were called squatters. Squatters were people who did not own the land on which they lived.

Most early squatters made their homes along the Ohio River. Some had come down the Ohio River from Pennsylvania and Virginia. Others had crossed the Ohio River from Kentucky.

Not long after the Indiana Territory was formed in 1800, many people of the Quaker religion came from the slave state of North Carolina to the Indiana Territory. One of their reasons for coming was that they did not believe in slavery. Because slavery in Indiana Territory was not allowed by the Ordinance of 1787, the Quakers traveled to the Indiana Territory. They settled in the upper parts of the Whitewater Valley, in southeast Indiana.

Where They Came From

Many of Indiana's first settlers came from the slave states of Tennessee, Kentucky, Virginia and the Carolinas. Others came from the free states of Pennsylvania, New York and New Jersey. Later settlers came across the Atlantic Ocean from England, Ireland and Germany.

How They Got Here

Some of the earliest settlers came from the southern states on a trail that Daniel Boone, the great woodsman from Pennsylvania, had cut through the wilderness. The trail was called Boone's Wilderness Road, and it led from Virginia across the Cumberland Gap to the middle of Kentucky.

On its eastern end, Boone's Wilderness Road joined an earlier trail that led south from Pennsylvania. This trail was called the Great Road. Many of the early settlers from Pennsylvania and New York took the Great Road and Boone's Wilderness Road to the land that later became Indiana.

Another trail that led toward Indiana was called Braddock's Road. This trail was built during the French and Indian War by the soldiers of a British general, Edward Braddock. The soldiers had cut the trail through the wilderness so that they could reach the French and drive them out of the Ohio region.

Braddock's Road led west from Maryland to a point on the Ohio River. Many years later, Braddock's Road became a part of the great National Road . . . the first wagon road that led west from the eastern United States into Indiana.

A short distance north of Braddock's Road was Forbes's Road, a trail that led from the middle of Pennsylvania to the Ohio River at Pittsburgh.

Both of these roads passed through the same region. Travelers from Pennsylvania used Forbes's Road, while travelers from Virginia used Braddock's Road.

Once he had arrived at the Ohio River in Pittsburgh, a settler could load his family, his household goods and his hogs on a flatboat. From Pittsburgh, the flatboat could float with the river current all the way to Indiana, as the Ohio River was the southern boundary of Indiana.

A flatboat was a strong, flat, wooden boat that could carry a heavy load. For many years during the early settlement of Indiana, the flatboat played an important part. It not only brought settlers to Indiana; it also gave the settlers a way to take their crops and hogs to the market town of New Orleans, at the mouth of the Mississippi River.

The First Landowners

Not long after the Treaty of Greenville in 1795, the United States offered to sell more of its Northwest Territory land to the settlers. It was the Indian land that Anthony Wayne had won for the United States by the Treaty of Greenville. Congress priced this

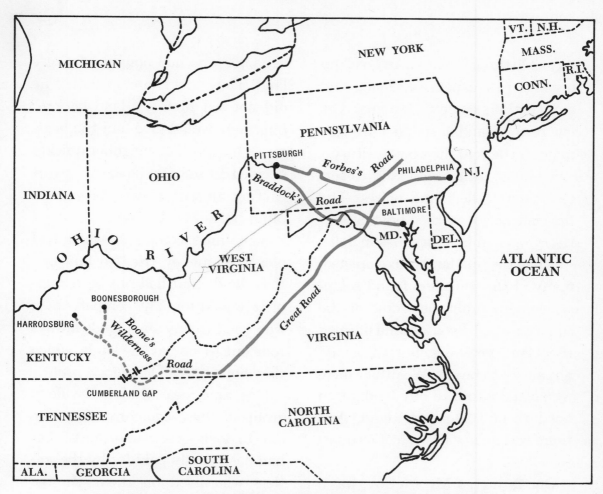

Major pioneer roads leading west: Forbes's Road, Braddock's Road,
The Great Road and Boone's Wilderness Road.

land, too, at $1.00 an acre, which everyone thought was a reasonable amount of money to pay. But since Congress once again insisted that no less than 640 acres had to be bought at one time, land buyers faced the same problem as before.

When William Henry Harrison was made governor of the Indiana Territory in 1800, the settlers soon found that he was a man who understood their problems. With William Henry Harrison's help, a new law was passed that allowed any settler to buy only 320 acres at $2.00 an acre. But even more important was the fact that the new law said a settler did not have to pay all the money at once. He could make payments over a four-year period. That way, a settler could make his farm pay for itself as he worked his land.

By 1804, a settler could buy as little as 160 acres. By 1820, he could buy as little as 80 acres. And as land became less expensive, more and more settlers came to Indiana. The low price of land in Indiana brought many settlers to the new territory.

The places that sold land to settlers were called land offices. The first land office in the Indiana Territory opened in Vincennes in 1804.

When the first land offices opened, many of the squatters found themselves with problems. Some of the squatters had lived on and farmed their land for years, but still could not afford to buy it. Wealthier men, who could afford to buy land, often tried to buy squatters' land. And there was no law to protect a squatter's land.

One farmer, a Mr. McCoy, was a squatter on a good piece of land in southwestern Indiana. He had always planned to buy his land, and he had built it into a very good farm. What was more, his neighbors liked him.

By borrowing fifty dollars, McCoy finally had enough money to buy his land. But when he went to the land office in Vincennes to buy the land, he learned that a neighbor of his had already bought it.

When some of McCoy's friendlier neighbors found out what had happened, they paid a visit to the neighbor who had bought McCoy's land. They told the man that if he did not sell McCoy's land back to him, they would give him the beating of his life. The neighbor quickly decided to sell the land to Farmer McCoy. In such a way, the settlers often helped each other.

Sometimes, companies which had plenty of money tried to buy settlers' lands that had not been completely paid for. The company men who tried to buy such lands always rode out to look at the lands, which they hoped to sell later for a profit.

One time, near Crawfordsville, a group of these company men rode out to look over some lands that had been partly paid for by the settlers who lived on them. As the company men looked at the lands, one of them noticed three bands of whooping Indians riding straight for him and his company friends. The Indians were in full war dress, and they were firing their rifles. Their bullets whistled by the ears of the company men.

Badly frightened, the company men galloped quickly away, but the Indians chased them until they were all many miles away from where they had started. Then, the Indians rode back the way they had come. Once back where they had

THE ROUTE OF THE BUFFALO TRACE

started, they went to their homes and put their Indian clothes away. For they were not Indians at all. They were settlers who had found a way to scare the company men away from the lands they felt were theirs.

The Buffalo Trace

Although many early settlers had traveled to Indiana by the Ohio River or Boone's Wilderness Road, once inside Indiana they had to travel on rough trails made by Indians or animals. One of these early trails, or traces, was called the Buffalo Trace.

The Buffalo Trace is believed to have been made by great herds of buffalo, on their way to and from salty places in the ground. Such salty places were called salt licks, because buffalo, like most cattle, like to lick salty things.

The Buffalo Trace led from the New Albany area to Vincennes. Almost two thirds of the early Indiana settlers who lived west of Clarksville came by the Buffalo Trace.

The Indians often traveled on animal trails, and they used the Buffalo Trace. Daniel Boone himself had followed a trail first made

75

by buffalo when he cut his famous Wilderness Road.

In 1804 the Buffalo Trace was just a path about two feet wide in most places, and 114 miles long. A trip from Clarksville to Vincennes took at least three days, and there was no grocery store or stable along the way. A traveler had to carry his own food and feed his horse from whatever grew along the Trace. Today we can drive from Clarksville to Vincennes in a few hours.

Indians made the early traces dangerous. Even after the Buffalo Trace became United States land, the Indians were a danger to travelers. In 1807, an entire family of settlers was attacked by Indians. After that, United States soldiers patrolled the Buffalo Trace. And for a while, the Indians left travelers alone.

Among the United States soldiers who used the Buffalo Trace was Lieutenant Josiah Bacon. He had been ordered to Vincennes to fight under Governor Harrison in the battle of Tippecanoe, and he had brought his wife to Vincennes with him. After the battle, Lieutenant Bacon, his wife and a few soldiers traveled along the Buffalo Trace from Vincennes to Louisville, Kentucky, which was across the Ohio River from the town of Clarksville.

The Bacons were lucky enough to ride on horseback. Lieutenant Bacon's wife, Lydia, kept a record of her trip. On the second day of her journey, she wrote:

"I like traveling on horseback and slept finely on the ground last night for the first time in my life, with a bearskin for our bedstead and a buffalo robe for a bed."

Later, Lydia Bacon wrote: "It rained hard all day yesterday. I never slept better than last night. We are now ready to start. I wish you could see us. It is funny to see the things that are done. I have a large bag on my saddle. In it are a Bible and a huge sponge cake given to us by friends before we left.

"Today the sun is bright, and everyone is healthy and cheerful. But it hurts me to see some of the poor soldiers' wives walking. Sometimes the mud is up to their knees, and some of them are carrying little children. We saw two houses, one of them empty. The settlers had been frightened away by the Indians."

During the journey, one of the soldiers sickened and died.

"He is buried in the woods in a bark coffin," wrote Lydia Bacon. "It was the best we could do."

Lydia Bacon did not write about

Cougars could be as dangerous as Indians.

another danger of the Buffalo Trace and of other trails like it. The danger was the cougar, a large cat-like, wild animal.

A full-grown cougar weighs about 150 pounds. Its sharp teeth, strong jaws and razor-like claws can easily kill a man. For one meal, a cougar eats almost eight pounds of meat. Cougars usually attack animals smaller than themselves. But when they are very hungry, they will attack animals three or four times their size.

At times, cougars crouched in trees that hung over the early trails. Travelers had to keep their eyes open to avoid becoming a cougar's meal. Cougars could be as dangerous as the Indians.

During the War of 1812, William Henry Harrison sent 150 men to protect travelers along the Buffalo Trace. But not until after the war, when the Indians had been beaten, was the Buffalo Trace really safe for travelers. Then farms and small towns grew up along the Buffalo Trace.

Other Early Trails

One of the Indian trails used by early settlers led from Fort Wayne past Terre Haute and on into the Illinois Territory. Another of the old trails followed the Whitewater

Valley north and then west to the Maumee River in northeastern Indiana.

There were many other Indian trails used by settlers. Many years later, some of these trails became the wide roads that are used today.

Of course, the settlers needed more trails than the Indians had made. The settlers made many of their own trails, which were called blaze trails.

Blaze trails were marked through the forest by gashes cut in trees with an ax. By following a blaze trail, a settler could go through a dark forest without becoming lost.

Why Settlers Needed Roads in Indiana

If a traveler walked or rode a horse to Indiana, a narrow path was wide enough. But once he settled and began to farm his land, he needed a way to haul his crops to a river where they could be taken by flatboat to a market town.

As settlers learned better ways of farming and as their crops grew larger, the crops had to be taken to a river by wagon. A wagon needed a wider trail than a man or horse. Wagons needed real roads.

Unless a settler could get his crops to market, he would have no money to take care of his family or to pay for his land. That is why roads were so important to the settlers.

Crossing Rivers

In 1800, there was not one bridge over an Indiana river. But settlers found ways to cross rivers. One way was by wading across at a ford. A ford was a shallow place in the river. Many of the Indian trails and blaze trails crossed rivers at fords. Sometimes, many trails met at a good ford.

Some of the larger Indiana rivers were too deep to cross by fording. To cross these rivers, a settler and his family often had to build a log raft. Then, with long poles cut from trees, they pushed the raft across the river. Once across the river, a settler tied the raft to a tree so that the raft could be used again.

As more and more settlers poured into Indiana, ferryboats began to appear. An early ferryboat was a strong wooden raft large enough to carry many people and their belongings. A ferryman at a much-used river crossing could make his living by charging settlers to take them across the river.

On smaller rivers, ferryboats were sometimes hooked to a rope

A pioneer ferryboat

stretched across a river and tied to a tree on each side of the river. In that way, the river current could not carry the ferryboat downstream as it was poled across a river.

Today, there are still a few ferryboats on the Wabash and Ohio rivers. But these ferryboats are moved by powerful engines, not by poles.

The First Steamboat On the Ohio River

In the year 1811, the settlers who lived along the Ohio River saw a strange and wonderful boat moving down the river. The boat had a large paddlewheel on each side, and it was much larger than a ferryboat. As the paddlewheels turned, pushing the boat along, fire and black smoke poured from the two large pipes that rose above the boat.

The strange new boat, which was called the *New Orleans*, frightened a few of the settlers. But others knew that the boat was a steamboat, with an engine of its own. They knew that this boat could go upstream almost as easily as it could go downstream.

Something the settlers probably did not know was that, in the coming years, other boats like the *New Orleans* would help make many changes in Indiana.

Some Early Towns

Because most of the early trails into Indiana led into southern Indiana, most of the early towns grew up along or near the Ohio River. Some of these early towns were Madison, New Albany, Lawrenceburg, Corydon, Jeffersonville and Charlestown.

Other early Indiana towns grew up along rivers that flowed into the Ohio River. That was because river travel was easier than traveling over the heavily-forested and often swampy land.

After the War of 1812

When the War of 1812 ended, many people in the eastern and southern United States knew that the Indian danger was past. Then greater numbers of settlers than ever came to the Indiana Territory.

In 1815, there were nearly 64,000 settlers in the great new Indiana Territory. In 1800, there had been only 2,500 settlers. So in 15 years, the number of settlers grew by more than twenty-five times.

10

How the Pioneers Lived

The Forest—Friend and Enemy

To us, a forest is a thing of living beauty. We enjoy hiking along woodland trails, or fishing in quiet streams, or picnicking under shady trees. But to the pioneer, it was something more. It was a challenge.

In many ways, the forest was his friend. For from it came all the things he needed to stay alive in the wilderness. His cabin, many of his tools, much of his food and clothing came from the forest.

In other ways, the forest was his enemy. For in it were things to fear. Wild animals and unfriendly Indians lived in the forest, too. And always there was the struggle to cut back the forest, so that corn and other crops could be planted.

Sometimes it took years before a pioneer had a farm. For just clearing the forest was very hard work. The heavier work was done by the father, but the mother and the children helped, too. There was something for everybody to do.

After a temporary cabin was built, the family would start work on making the first clearing. The small trees and bushes would be cut first and burned. The children and mother could do this. Then the father would start cutting down the

81

Logrolling on a pioneer farm

Girdling trees on a pioneer farm

big trees. To do this job a good woodsman had to be strong and skillful. He used an ax, which he had to sharpen often. Usually trees were cut down in the winter, when other farm work could not be done.

In the late winter or early spring, there would be a logrolling. A pioneer would invite his neighbors to come and help him. The men would make a game of it. Teams were formed, and each team tried to work faster than the others. The logs were rolled into big piles and burned. But the best logs were saved for the new cabin.

Logrolling was fun, but it was also hard work. After the logrolling was over, the women would serve a big picnic dinner.

Sometimes, the pioneer would "girdle" the big trees instead of cutting them down. This meant that the bark of the trees was cut away in a ring. Trees girdled this way died, but it took many months. The pioneer would plant hills of corn among the dying trees.

While the work of clearing fields went on, a man had to keep a sharp lookout for Indians. The Indians did not like to see the woods cut down. They could not hunt deer where the white man planted corn. The pioneer also had to watch for wolves and bears because they attacked the farm animals.

This was the forest as an enemy.

Good Things Come From the Forest

But from this same forest, a man got wood to build his cabin and his barn. He had all the wood he needed to fence in his ground. But it was hard work to split the rails needed for a fence.

He was able to make the furniture and tools he needed. With an ax and a knife, a man could make almost anything. He made beds and chairs and tables, as well as buckets and barrels. His wife had to have something to churn the butter in. And of course she could not do without her spinning wheel. Even the wagon they used to drive to the nearest settlement was made by hand—frame, body, wheels and all.

Until a man could put up a permanent house, he and his family might live in what was called a pole shed. This shed had three walls, made from branches and poles. Dried grass was plastered between the branches with mud, to keep the wind and rain out. The fourth side, which faced south, was left open.

The family slept on the ground inside the pole shed, on beds made

A pole shed

from dry leaves. They covered themselves with bearskins or furs from other wild animals of the forest. For cooking and warmth, a log fire was kept burning day and night just outside the open side.

In nice weather, this kind of camping was pleasant. But when winter winds blew rain and snow in through the open side, or filled the shed with smoke from the fire, the family had a rough time. A pioneer would try to build the permanent cabin before winter.

Building the Cabin

The cabins themselves were made from heavy logs cut to the same length. Big rocks were put in each corner, to raise the cabin off the ground. The heavy logs were then lifted, one over the other, until the cabin was about eight logs high. The ends of the logs were cut out in such a way that the other logs would fit exactly into the cut ends. This was most important, for most of the settlers had to build their cabins without the use of a single nail.

There were open places where the snow would blow in.

One pioneer told his grandson, "There was plenty of open places under the roof where the snow would blow in sometimes. But that didn't matter much. If you slept in the loft, you just pulled your head under the covers during a storm. When you got up in the morning, you shook the snow off the covers, grabbed your shirt and britches, and hopped down the ladder to the fireplace, where it was good and warm."

There was usually only one window. Greased paper was used to cover it. The paper kept the snow and rain out, but let the light in.

There were no keys or locks. Instead, a latch was put on the doors. The latch was just a long wooden bar across the middle of the door. A leather string was pushed or pulled through a hole made in the door above the latch. At night, or when Indians were near, the leather string was pulled inside. Then the latch could not be opened from the outside.

At all other times, the latchstring hung outside, so the latch could be lifted. When a pioneer said, "The latchstring is out," it was his way of saying, "You are welcome to my house."

At one end of the cabin was a large fireplace. It was the most important part of the cabin, for it was the kitchen and the heating system all at the same time.

In building his cabin, the first thing the settler looked for was water. If he could find a spring, he would build as close to it as he could. It was the children's job to go to the spring and bring water to the cabin. Where there were no springs, wells had to be dug.

Working the Land

Working the land was even harder than putting up the cabin. Under the cleared ground, there were roots that were almost impossible to dig out. Even where there was a prairie, turning the ground was not easy. The grass roots were tough and deep. Often the dirt would stick to the plow, so that it had to be scraped off again and again. Plowing the ground was a hard job.

The settlers were not expert farmers. They did not know too much about working the land. Sometimes the weeds grew as high as the corn. Hoeing the corn by hand was a job for the boys and sometimes for the girls, too.

Many settlers raised cattle, sheep and hogs, as well as crops. Cattle gave them milk and meat, and sheep gave them wool. And the animals could be sold, or traded, for things the settlers needed and could not make themselves.

The Pennsylvania Rifle

One thing that helped solve many of the settler's problems was the Pennsylvania rifle, sometimes called the Kentucky rifle. With it, a settler could shoot the deer he needed to put fresh meat on the family table. He could protect himself against hungry wolves, cougars and angry bears. Most important of all, he could defend himself and his family against the Indians.

About 55 inches long and weighing from 8 to 10 pounds, the Pennsylvania rifle could kill a man or animal at 300 yards. It was loaded from the end of its long barrel. First, powder from a powder horn was poured down the barrel. Then, a lead bullet wrapped in a piece of greased skin was pushed down the barrel with a wooden ramrod. When the trigger was pulled, sparks from a flint set off the powder.

The Pennsylvania rifle was such a fine weapon that it was used for nearly 100 years. Washington's soldiers used it in the French and Indian War and in the Revolutionary War. Daniel Boone carried one most of his life. The Pennsylvania rifle helped America win its freedom, feed its settlers and make the land safe.

Making Clothes

While the settler was clearing the land, his wife was kept very busy around the home. She made the clothes the family wore. First she spun the yarn. Then she wove the cloth from which the clothes were made. Summer clothing was made from flax; winter clothing was made with wool taken from the sheep.

At first the men wore shirts made from deerskin, just as the Indians did. Leggings were made from buckskin, fringed down along the legs, Indian-style. But after a while, the men wore shirts from cloth woven by the women. The front part of the shirt was very loose. When the pioneer put his belt on, he used the front part of his shirt to carry whatever he needed. It was like having an enormous pocket. His hunting knife was placed in a loop in his belt.

Men wore fur hats in winter. In summer, hats were made out of straw. Women wore cloth bonnets. Moccasins were usually made by

the father. Boots and shoes were bought from a traveling shoemaker or in the nearest town. They were for winter use. Sometimes a pioneer father would make shoes, too. In summer everyone went barefoot. One pioneer said: "Shoes for us boys came last. Sometimes Pap didn't get to us bigger boys until pretty late in the fall. I guess he thought it made us tough and healthy to go barefoot in the frost. As I was the oldest boy, it would be up toward Christmas before I got any shoes. Sometimes us older boys would go to school half a term barefooted. On frosty mornings in the fall we heated a clapboard before the fireplace until it was almost charred, stuck it under our arm and ran through the frost until our feet began to sting. Then we threw the clapboard on the ground, stood on it until our feet warmed, grabbed it up and made another run."

For the girls, shoes were "Sunday best" for church. They carried their stockings and shoes until they caught sight of the church. Then they would put their shoes and stockings on quickly. But as soon as they left the church, they would take them off again. They loved getting dressed up. But they were more comfortable carrying their shoes.

Cooking the Food

Pioneer women didn't have shiny new electric or gas stoves to cook on. All the food was cooked over the fire in the fireplace.

"I remember," a settler told his grandson, "sometimes a few ashes would get in the cooking. But that didn't matter. We thought it just helped season it some. Mush and milk was a common meal at supper time, and fried mush for breakfast. Many a time us children went to bed on a supper of mush and milk and not a thing else."

There was plenty to eat besides mush and milk, however. The forest was a rich source for meat. The men in the family would hunt deer and other animals in the forest. When they got tired of deer meat, the mother might say to her husband, or one of her sons, "Go out and get me a turkey." And it was as easy as that, for turkeys were plentiful.

To get sugar, the pioneers tapped the maple trees, just as the Indians did. Sugar making in the woods in the early spring was a time the children enjoyed.

The women took care of the small gardens, in which they raised potatoes and pumpkins and other vegetables. They raised tomatoes,

Pioneer cooking

Tapping maple trees for sugar sap.

87

too, but they never thought of eating them. Tomatoes were called love apples. It was thought if you ate one it would poison you. But tomatoes were pretty to look at. So they were brought into the house for decoration.

Fun and Games

Everyone in the house worked, even the children. But time was found for fun, too. The men and boys often played rough games to show how strong they were. "Rastlin'" was a favorite sport. There were running and jumping contests. Both men and boys pitched horseshoes and played ball and games like leapfrog and roll the hoop. Many of the games they played were copied from the Indians. But most of all the men enjoyed showing off their skill in shooting. In a shooting match, a man could show what a keen eye he had. He could be proud of his shooting, for his rifle meant the difference between life and death on the frontier. His rifle gave him food on the table and protected his home from the Indians.

The women did not take part in these games. While the men played, the women visited with each other. They had quilting parties, spinning parties, cooking parties and even chicken-plucking parties. Their parties were different from the games the men played, for as the women enjoyed each other's company, they were also getting their work done.

Cornhuskings were very popular with all the people. Corn was piled high in a barn. Then everyone was invited to come and husk it. A game was made of it, with everyone there chosen to be on one side or the other. The pile of corn was divided. At the signal, everyone began to husk the corn. The side that finished first won. After all the corn was husked, everyone helped clear up the barn. Then there was a barn dance. Fiddlers played, and one of the men called out the dance steps. Girls might sing tunes like:

I am too young, I am not fit,
I cannot leave my mamma yet.

Or the boys and girls might sing:

Old Dan Tucker's a fine old
   man,
Washed his feet in the frying
   pan,
Combed his hair with a wagon
   wheel,
And died with a tooth-ache in
   his heel.

Square
Dance

Spelling Bee

Quilting
Party

Wrestling Contest

Or the caller might say:

The cat's in the buttermilk,
skip-to-my-Lou,
The cat's in the buttermilk,
skip-to-my-Lou,
The cat's in the buttermilk,
skip-to-my-Lou,
Skip-to-my-Lou, my darling.

Weddings were just as popular. In those days, weddings were neighborhood affairs. When a wedding was planned, the bride's father would go from house to house. "There's going to be a wedding at my house Tuesday," he might say.

That was all anyone needed to hear! The women in the neighbor-

hood would all go to the bride's house at once. They would start cooking all the food for the wedding dinner. Meanwhile, the men would get together and help the young bridegroom build a cabin. In a few days, his cabin would be ready.

Feasting would go on for hours on the day of the wedding. People came from miles and miles around, all dressed up, except for their shoes. These they would put on just before they reached the house where the wedding was taking place. If there was a spring or river nearby, they would wash their feet before they put their shoes on.

When the young couple moved into their new cabin, the neighbors held a "shivaree." People would come around late at night, and bang on pots and pans or shoot in the air, and laugh and shout for hours. Everyone had fun at the "shivaree" except the young couple, who had to put up with all the noise!

Sunday Meetings and Get-Togethers

Pioneers looked forward all week to Sunday meetings at the church. It was a time for dressing up in one's best clothes. Everyone went to church to pray, but after the services, men, women and children visited with each other.

When special meetings were held, people came from miles around. The women brought food. Some brought baskets of fried chicken. Others brought cakes and pies. Tablecloths were spread on the grass in the shade of the trees. It was a happy time for everyone.

Pioneers used almost any reason for a get-together. They went to funerals as well as weddings. They enjoyed church camp meetings or political meetings. Everyone looked forward to a trip into the nearest town, especially on court day. They enjoyed hearing the lawyers argue the cases. In town, people visited with each other and took care of their trading at the same time.

Spelling bees were held. But not only the children took part in them. Spelling was a game and a challenge to grownups as well. It was an honor to win a prize as the best speller. A good speller was the talk of the

Sometimes "Granny cure" medicine tasted horrible.

neighborhood. If you were a good speller, people knew about you for miles and miles!

How Pioneer Children Played

There were toys for the children, but they were almost always home-made. For girls, mothers made rag dolls and balls made from yarn. For boys, fathers made sleds, bows and arrows and whistles.

And of course both boys and girls had all the pets they wanted. They had dogs and lambs and goats and other animals. Often they made pets of wild animals in the forest, such as raccoons.

Their playground was all the great outdoors. It did not take long for a child to learn woodcraft.

"Granny" Cures

Pioneers did have some good

times, in spite of all their hard work. But at other times, sickness kept them from doing anything at all. Even though pioneers were out in the fresh, open air, they got sick often.

They had no idea of sanitation. Chickens, ducks, pigs and dogs wandered in and out of houses. There were no screens to keep the flies out. It was not surprising that many people became ill.

When someone was sick, home remedies or "granny" cures were tried.

If someone had a stomachache, he put his feet in hot ashes mixed with water. Then he got into bed and put boiled ears of corn on his stomach to keep it warm.

To cure a sore throat, pepper was sprinkled on a piece of fat and tied around the neck. Or else goose grease was rubbed in all around the throat. Spring fever could be cured by eating hailstones, or drinking water from snow in March.

If a person drank something that tasted horrible, it was thought to be a sure cure for whatever he had. The worse it tasted, the better it was for whatever was wrong, whether it was the measles or a fever or just a cold.

If a man needed glasses, he did not go to a doctor. He just went to a village general store. Or else he waited until a peddler came to the house. Then he would try on glasses until he found a pair he liked.

If he had a toothache, he took medicine. If that didn't help, he tied one end of a string around his tooth. The other end he tied to the branch of a young tree. When he let go of the branch, it snapped back in the air. Usually his tooth would snap out at the same time.

Pioneer School Days

In pioneer days children did not always go to school. Often there was no school to attend. Or sickness kept a child from going. And when he was feeling fine, he had many chores to do. Very often, the parents thought the chores were more important than school.

A school was usually built by those parents who wanted their children to go. To get to the school, the children often walked miles through the woods. Or they might ride to school on horseback.

The school was a one-room log cabin, to which about twenty children came. A big fireplace at one end of the cabin was used for heating. The teacher, or schoolmaster, as he was called, had a chair and a table. The children sat on benches. They had no desks.

Reading, writing, arithmetic and spelling were studied. The children used little slates to write on most of the time. But sometimes they went to the "writing desk" and wrote on paper with pen and ink. They made their own pens, from the quills of a turkey or some other bird. A quill was a long, stiff feather taken from the wing or tail of a bird. The hard part of the feather was sharpened to a point. Ink was made from the juice of berries.

School started early in the morning. Children of all ages were in the same classroom. First came arithmetic. But arithmetic was not as important as writing or spelling. The schoolmaster called each child in turn to read out of the spelling book. Each child went as far in the book as he wished to go.

He danced around like a wild man.

Here is what one settler remembered about his school days: "Mr. Hawkins lived in a double cabin with just his wife at home. That gave him room to hold school in his kitchen. Even though it was a long trip through the dense woods, Pap signed for us. Master Hawkins was a big fat man, jolly and good natured. He let us do about as we pleased. I guess we learned a little at that. If the weather was bad at noon, we sat around where we pleased to eat our dinner. Anything like a nice day and we went outside to eat. I don't think there were more than twelve of us going to that school.

"Something funny happened at school, when the sun was warming things up. Master Hawkins had a habit of sitting in the doorway during the noon hour when the sun shone down nice and warm and taking a nap. We were playing around out in front of the cabin, when someone noticed a frog hopping along pretty close to the master. We soon saw the cause of its hurry when a garter snake came crawling along. The master always wore buckskin britches that stood out at the bottom like a sailor's trousers.

"Well, the frog spied the master's legs sticking out there on the ground and those big open britches, which I guess he took for a hollow log. In he went for a good place to hide. That cold frog on the master's bare leg was mighty awakening, for he grabbed his britches leg with both hands and danced around like a wild man. We tried to tell him what it was, but he couldn't hear anything. We all had a good laugh at the master, and he took it in good humor. But we noticed he didn't take any more naps in an open door."

So it was the pioneers spent their early days on the frontier. As the years went by and more people settled on the land, life became easier for the settler.

Pioneer Transportation

Indians followed animal trails and used canoes on rivers and lakes.

Pioneer scouts cut through the forests to make new trails and roads.

On land, pioneer settlers first followed Indian trails on foot. Later, they traveled by horse, and finally, as trails were widened, by wagon.

Many pioneer settlers traveled to Indiana on flatboats, which they floated down the Ohio River from the eastern states.

11

Trails and Rivers, Roads and Canals

The Importance of Transportation

Today everyone travels quite easily in cars, planes and trains. A trip across Indiana is hardly a trip at all. It is easy to forget that it once took days to cross the state—days of hard travel.

Today farmers ship crops to market easily by truck or train. And these same crops are sometimes shipped across the seas by airplane or steamship. But there was a time not long ago when farmers had trouble finding buyers for their crops because they had no quick, easy way to ship them.

Transportation is one of a country's greatest needs. A country that can transport goods and people can grow. But a country without transportation cannot.

Transportation can work magic. It can change a piece of nearly worthless goods into a valuable one. For example, beavers were common in Indiana years ago. But their pelts were of little value in Indiana, because there were no fur coats being made then in the state of Indiana.

In France and England, however, there was a great demand for beaver pelts which could be made into expensive fur coats. When the low-cost beaver pelts from Indiana were shipped to Europe, they became much more valuable.

Transportation also changes the cost of goods in other ways. If a seller can send a large amount at a lower rate, then he can afford to sell his goods for less. If a fur trader could ship 300 beaver pelts at one time, he could sell them for less than if he could ship only 50. The reason is simple. If he could ship 300 at once, the shipping company would charge him less per pelt than if he shipped 50 at six different times.

So transportation is important not only in getting goods from one place to another, but it also helps set the final price of the goods.

To grow, a country must also be able to move its people. The wilderness could never have been overcome if settlers could not have made their way to the frontier. And as time went on they had to move many kinds of materials to their far-flung homesteads. Without the ability to move building materials and workers, Hoosiers would still live in the wilderness. Indiana, like all states, was able to grow and become wealthy only as its transportation system grew.

Prehistoric Transportation

Since man first appeared on earth he has had the problem of moving himself and his belongings from one place to another. Prehistoric men had poor transportation. It took them thousands of years even to discover how to make and use wheels. When early man wanted to move something from one place to another, he had to carry or drag it. When he traveled he had to thread his way through forests and wade through swamps, streams and rivers. At best he could sometimes follow animal trails.

The prehistoric Indians who lived in Indiana were much like the prehistoric people who lived in other parts of the world. The men were hunters and walked along animal trails to find game and water. The women wandered along the trails looking for plants and firewood. When men killed an animal, they had to drag or carry it back to the camp. Women dragged or carried plants and firewood.

Prehistoric man lived as he did partly because he could not move

things easily and because he could not travel long distances easily. His life was limited by where he could go and what he could take with him when he went.

Indians of Indiana

The Indians who lived in Indiana when the white settlers came did not yet have horses. But they used canoes for traveling on streams and rivers and lakes. The waterways, in fact, were the Indians' roads. They could travel long distances by water.

Of course, no single stream or river would always take the Indians where they wanted to go. Often they had to change from a lake to a river, or from a stream to a lake. They could easily carry their light canoes from one waterway to another.

The paths the Indians made from one waterway to another were called portages. The early French explorers in Indiana also used these Indian portages. Portages were an important part of the first transportation system in what later became Indiana.

Animal trails made up the other part of the earliest transportation system. Like the prehistoric Indians, the later ones also used the

animal trails as roads. These narrow paths became more and more worn over the years, worn by men and animals alike.

How the Settlers Traveled

After the Revolution, American settlers poured into the old Northwest and into the area that would become Indiana. Many came along the National Road which started in Maryland.

Wagons were the first traffic on the National Road. These wagons were large and heavy and were covered with wooden hoops. Over the hoops was stretched cloth or canvas, to keep out the rain and dust.

The large wagons were pulled by four or six horses called Conestoga (kŏn′ə-stō′gə) horses. And the covered wagons, which were named after the horses that pulled them, were called Conestoga wagons.

Conestoga wagons were made with hand tools. The wagons were built of wood and were about sixteen feet long by four feet wide. Each wooden wheel, four feet high, had a tire made of an iron hoop.

At one time, pioneer traffic seemed to move along the National Road in an endless stream. It was an exciting thing to see and hear. The wagon horses all had bells that could be heard jangling half a mile away. The family dogs barked as they ran along. And the family cow, tied to the wagon, mooed loudly because she had to walk so fast.

The National Road was one of the best roads of the day. Built by the federal government, it was macadamized (mə-kăd′ə-mīzd′) and was 30 feet wide. Macadamized road, invented by a Scottish engineer named John L. McAdam, was crushed or broken stone laid on a

Pioneer traffic moved along

wet earthen bed and packed down.

The settlers in Indiana were quick to use the animal trails already worn and widened by the Indians. The settlers, however, had strong horses and oxen, and their wagons contained heavy loads of household goods.

When it rained, the Indian trails turned to mud. The settlers' heavy animals and wagons sank deep into the sticky stuff. It sometimes took hours of hard work just to move a few yards along a muddy path. Sometimes the paths were too narrow, and the settlers had to stop and chop down trees or remove other obstacles.

the National Road in an endless stream.

The animal and Indian trails on the Indiana side of the Ohio were very different from the National Road. But the settlers did the best they could. As the territory grew, road work got underway.

Road Surfaces

There were several ways to improve road surfaces besides macadamizing. One kind of early road surface was made by chopping down trees and, after trimming the limbs, laying them side by side. This was usually done only over short distances. In fact, this method was used mainly across low places where water pooled in wet weather and made the road hard to travel.

This kind of surface was called corduroy (kôr′də-roi′) road. Corduroy roads were very bumpy. They were hard for horses to walk on and they made wagons shake violently.

Another kind of surfacing used smooth-cut planks instead of logs. Plank roads were a better attempt to make travel easier and more pleasant. Plank roads were smoother than corduroy roads, but they had their own bad features. They quickly became covered with dirt. When rain fell, the planks were so slippery the horses could hardly pull the wagons.

Broken stone or gravel roads were best. Gravel packed down well and made a hard, smooth surface. And water ran off or through the stones quickly.

The First Good Roads

A number of short roads were built early in the history of the Indiana Territory. But the first important roads were not built until long after Indiana became a state in 1816.

One of these major roads, at first made of planks and later graveled, was the National, or Cumberland, Road. It was part of the National Road which had been built by the federal government.

When completed, the National Road in Indiana joined Terre Haute, near the western border, with Richmond, on the eastern boundary. It passed through Indianapolis at the center of the state. This road took ten years to build and was finished in 1839.

Another important road was the Michigan Road. This road was built about the same time as the Indiana portion of the National Road. It ran north from the Ohio River at Madison through Indianapolis to Michigan City on Lake Michigan.

The Stagecoach

Once roads were built, travel across the state became heavier. Among the most important means of transportation was the stagecoach.

Traveling by stagecoach was an adventure for anyone who made a trip. Crossing the state could take three days or more. The roads were rough and bumpy. Sometimes the coaches got stuck in heavy mud. Often the passengers had to help push them out.

Many passengers carried pistols because of robbers. These highwaymen would stop stagecoaches and take anything of value. They sometimes took mail sacks or packages of freight. They also took money, watches and jewelry from the passengers.

The stagecoach was like a car or bus today. It was a good way to carry a few people and a small amount of baggage from one place to another. But for hauling large amounts of freight, a different kind of transportation was needed.

The Waterways

From the time settlers began to arrive in Indiana, the waterways were important. One of the main waterways was Indiana's biggest river, the Ohio.

Settlers often came down the Ohio on flatboats. They could float their possessions, families and even some animals on the barge-like boats. When they came to a likely-looking spot, they went ashore and made a homestead.

Floating down the Ohio was easier than making the overland journey by covered wagon. But settlers who came by water then had to settle near the river. Once the flatboat was unloaded, it was difficult to move household goods and animals for any distance overland. But land along the river was usually rich and fertile and good for farming. So the settlers were glad to settle on riverside land.

As the state grew, water transportation became even more important. Farmers shipped their crops to distant cities by boat. Water was, in fact, the only way to ship large amounts of goods easily. And for early water transportation, three kinds of boats were developed— flatboats, keelboats and canal boats.

Flatboats

Many kinds of boats were called flatboats. A simple raft was called a flatboat, as were barges and arks. Some flatboats resembled keelboats. But there was an important difference between flatboats and keelboats. Keelboats were made and run by businessmen to haul freight both up and downstream. Flatboats went only one way—downstream. And they were often built by farmers or anyone else who had freight to ship to a downstream port. When a flatboat had made its single run, it was finished. It was usually broken up and its wood sold.

There were other differences too between flatboats and keelboats. Flatboats had no sail as keelboats did. They used only the river's current for power, and the crew guided the boat with long poles. During spring in the first half of the 1800's, the Ohio and Mississippi rivers were crowded with flatboats loaded with grain and meat.

Flatboating was always an adventure. As the water rose during early spring, flatboat building began along many small streams in Indiana. When the melting snow and early rains had filled all the watercourses to the brim, the flatboaters would load their produce and begin exciting journeys to ports on one of the big rivers.

Each journey by flatboat was different, and there was always danger. Snags or rocks could upset a boat or tear it apart. River pirates sometimes surprised the crew and stole both boat and freight.

Then after the journey was over there was always the long trip home. This was made on foot or horseback or by stagecoach, depending on how successful the sale of crops and meat had been.

Keelboats and Keelboatmen

Keelboats were among the most important early boats on Indiana and neighboring waterways. Keelboats, which were developed from the bateaux (bă-tōz') used by the French, were long, narrow boats. They often used a sail to help move them upstream. They had a large wooden paddle, called a sweep, at the back. This was used to help guide the boat downstream.

Keelboats were run by businessmen to haul freight. They were important because they could go upstream more easily than most boats. And they could float in shallower water than most, too. They operated on both big rivers and small streams.

In going upstream, keelboats were poled by the crew if the wind was wrong for sailing. Four or five

Flatboat going downriver

Keelboat going upriver

men stood on each side of the deck with long poles. Each man placed one end of his pole against the bottom of the stream or river and then walked toward the rear of the boat while pushing hard against the pole. Poling was hard, slow work and only very strong men could do it. If there was room along the bank, the men sometimes got off the boat and pulled it with a tow rope.

Men who worked the keelboats were rough and tough. They often bragged about their strength. They were called half-horse and half-alligator. Among the most famous of them was a man named Mike Fink.

Mike Fink was a real person, but through time he has become a legend like Paul Bunyan. So many stories have been made up about him that it is hard to know which ones are true, or even partly true. Mike worked keelboats on the Ohio and Mississippi in the late 1700's and early 1800's. He was said to be the toughest man on the rivers. Like other keelboatmen he was fond of bragging about his strength and ability. But according to the legend, all Mike's bragging was absolutely true.

One story, surely made up, says that Mike once challenged six men on another boat to a race. He tied the tow rope around his waist and

Mike Fink wins race against six men.

jumped into the river. The six men on the other boat poled against the current as hard as they could, but Mike beat them easily.

Mike Fink later left the river and its boats and became a trapper. He was killed, so they say, in the north while playing a deadly game called "shoot the cup." In this game, two men would shoot drinking cups off each other's heads. Mike was known for his shooting skill, but this time he missed the cup and killed the other man. Friends of the slain man said Mike was too good with a gun to have missed accidentally. So they shot Mike. The prince of keelboatmen was dead.

Canals and Canal Boats

In Europe, canals were used to improve water transportation. Canals tied together many big watercourses. The same idea was being used in eastern America. The new state of Indiana needed canals too. With canals connecting the major rivers, water transportation in the state could be far more useful. Farmers who lived away from rivers or streams would also be able to float their crops to far-off markets.

Three big canals were planned for Indiana during the early years. Two of them were actually finished. One ran from Hagerstown, near the eastern border, down to the Ohio River. It was called the Whitewater Canal. Another ran from Fort Wayne to Terre Haute and on down to Evansville, connecting the Maumee River and the Ohio. This was the Wabash and Erie Canal. The third canal, which was never finished, was to have run through Indianapolis in central Indiana, connecting the Wabash and Erie Canal with the Whitewater Canal.

In addition, there were plans for canals to connect all these systems with Lake Michigan. But work was never begun on them.

For a time canal boats seemed to do their work well. Pulled by horses walking along the bank, these shallow riding boats could carry large amounts of freight. But canal boats were slow. And bad weather could cause banks to give way or cause such high water that the tow horses could not walk. At other times the water could fall so low that the boats had trouble getting through.

Of course, the worst problem with canals was that they could not be used in the wintertime.

In 1834, some of the leading citizens of Brookville learned in a surprising way about the problems of canal travel. They took a ride to see a newly-built section of the Whitewater canal. The water softened the fresh dirt of the banks. One of the banks caved in and all the water ran out. The travelers were left sitting on the muddy bottom of the empty canal. The state's effort to build a canal system caused serious money problems.

Steamboats

While keelboats, flatboats and canal boats were carrying much of the state's freight, a new kind of boat was beginning to appear on the rivers. In 1811 Nicholas Roosevelt had come west with his steamboat, the *New Orleans*. He had proved that steamboats could go down the Ohio and Mississippi to New Orleans, Louisiana.

The Indiana state government planned to make many Indiana waterways safe for steamboating. They hoped especially that the White and Wabash rivers could be cleared for this use. In April of 1831, a steamboat named the *Robert*

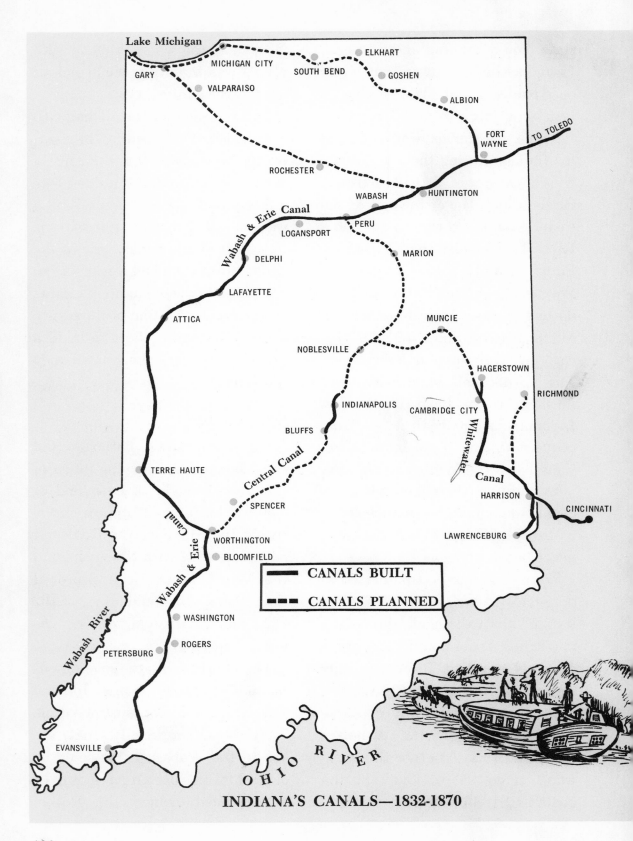

Lake Michigan

ELKHART

MICHIGAN CITY
SOUTH BEND
GOSHEN

GARY

VALPARAISO

ALBION

FORT
WAYNE

TO TOLEDO

ROCHESTER

HUNTINGTON

WABASH

Wabash & Erie Canal

PERU

LOGANSPORT

MARION

DELPHI

LAFAYETTE

MUNCIE

ATTICA

NOBLESVILLE

HAGERSTOWN

RICHMOND

INDIANAPOLIS

CAMBRIDGE CITY

BLUFFS

Whitewater

TERRE HAUTE

Central Canal

Canal

SPENCER

HARRISON

CINCINNATI

WORTHINGTON

LAWRENCEBURG

Wabash & Erie Canal

BLOOMFIELD

CANALS BUILT
CANALS PLANNED

Wabash River

WASHINGTON

ROGERS

PETERSBURG

EVANSVILLE

OHIO RIVER

INDIANA'S CANALS—1832-1870

Hanna actually did reach Indianapolis on White River, but this was one of the few successful steamboat runs on this river.

The Wabash was not a good steamboat river either. Like the White, it was often filled with trees and other debris. And there were shallows that the boats could barely get across even when the water was at its highest. Steamboats did continue to run on the Wabash for several years, however.

The best river by far was the Ohio. Many boats used the big river. It was a good river not only because it was wide and deep, but because it led directly to the Mississippi—the most important river for steamboats in the United States.

So in the years before 1850, Indiana already had a busy transportation system. It had several kinds of roads. It had water transportation on rivers, streams and canals. These methods of transportation were far from perfect, however.

Canal boats, pulled by horses walking on the bank, were slow. A person walking could often beat a canal boat to its destination by a day or more. Steamboat travel was little better. Steamboats seldom stayed on schedule, and steamboat captains sometimes refused to stop for passengers who had been waiting many hours or even days.

The stagecoach was the most reliable method of personal travel. Although the roads were rough or muddy, and in spite of robbers, the stagecoaches arrived at their stations usually on time. And they ran to many parts of the state where there were no waterways.

So there were ways to move goods to distant markets. There were ways for people to travel from one place to another. But all these methods of transporting people and goods had problems. Boats and barges could not run in the winter months. Stagecoaches were uncomfortable and expensive. A better method of transportation was needed.

The Coming of the Railroads

In the 1820's, men in the East had begun testing trains. Some early ones had been pulled by horses. Others had sails. But now these men were trying to equip trains with steam engines.

The steam engine quickly proved its worth, and the building of the railroads began. Here, everyone said, was a method of transportation that was far better than any-

Madison—Indianapolis Railroad train, 1847

thing before. If cars could run on rails and be pulled by an engine, they could run smoothly and on time. A train would not be bothered by bad weather or bad roads or any of the other things that hindered stagecoaches and boats.

The earliest railroad in the United States was built in the East about 1830. By 1834, Indiana had its first railroad. However, this first Indiana railroad was little more than a large toy. Built near Shelbyville, it was only a mile and a quarter long. This railroad did not actually connect any towns. It was really an experiment to see if railroads would work. People rode it only for fun. It did not have a steam locomotive either. Like early trains in the East, it was pulled by horses. But the railroad was on its way, and nothing could stop it.

In 1838, the state began a railroad from Madison to Indianapolis. Nine years later the track was finished and Indiana had its first steam-driven railroad train.

After that, many railroads were built. Some crossed the state and connected towns within it. Others connected Indiana with other states.

One of the earliest connected Indiana with Ohio, a state that had cooperated on a canal project in years gone by.

The canal systems which had once seemed so promising quickly fell by the way. They could not make enough money to support themselves. There was still some water traffic, but the railroad soon became by far the most important kind of transportation.

The railroads grew with each passing year. They were important not only in Indiana, but throughout the United States. The railroads tied the nation firmly together for the first time.

But the coming Civil War would stop the growth of railroads. The railroads and every other great plan would have to wait until the thunder of guns had died.

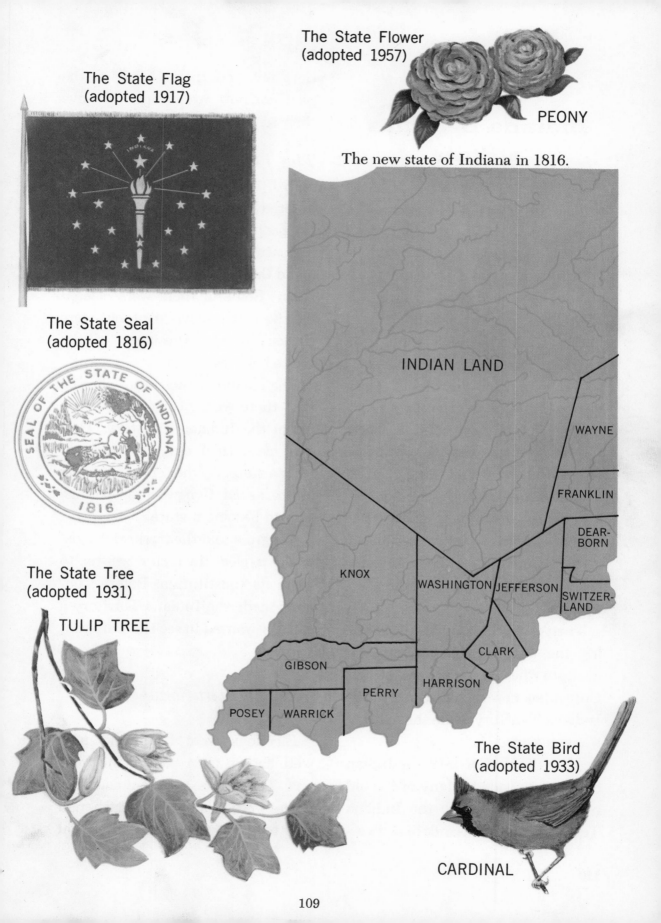

The State Flower
(adopted 1957)

PEONY

The State Flag
(adopted 1917)

The new state of Indiana in 1816.

The State Seal
(adopted 1816)

SEAL OF THE STATE OF INDIANA

1816

The State Tree
(adopted 1931)

TULIP TREE

INDIAN LAND

WAYNE

FRANKLIN

DEAR-
BORN

KNOX

WASHINGTON JEFFERSON

SWITZER-
LAND

CLARK

GIBSON

HARRISON

PERRY

POSEY WARRICK

The State Bird
(adopted 1933)

CARDINAL

12

Indiana Becomes a State

The Indiana Territory—1811

By 1811, a great many settlers in Indiana thought the territory should become a state. Since the Revolutionary War, five new states had been added to the original thirteen. Indiana people had good reasons for wanting statehood. They wanted to elect their governor and manage their own affairs. They wanted the greater independence that statehood would bring.

Under the Northwest Ordinance, a territory had to have at least 60,000 people in order to become a state. But in 1811, there were only 35,000 people in the Indiana Territory.

Then came the War of 1812. During the war, some settlers moved back to the safer, eastern states. Only a few new settlers came to the Indiana Territory while the fighting was going on.

After the War of 1812, the Indian danger was ended. Many of the old settlers came back to the Indiana Territory, and thousands of new set-

tlers followed them. Most of the pioneers now were eager to have their territory become a state.

The 1815 Census

In 1815, the territorial legislature ordered that a census, or count of the people, be made. The territorial legislature was a group of men who made the laws for the Indiana Territory. Some of them were elected by the settlers, while others were chosen by the President of the United States.

The results of the census showed that there were nearly 64,000 people in the Indiana Territory. That was more than enough people to form a state. So the territorial legislature asked Congress for permission to become a state.

Congress told the territorial legislature to elect the men it wanted to write its constitution. Before Congress made the Indiana Territory a state, it wanted to see the state constitution.

The Constitutional Convention

Elections were held, and men were chosen from each of the Indiana Territory's thirteen counties. There were 43 men in all. Each man was to go to Corydon, the capital of the Indiana Territory, to help write the state constitution.

Corydon was a small town about 20 miles north of the Ohio River. Corydon had been the capital of the Indiana Territory since 1813.

On a June day in 1816, the 43 men who had been elected met in a little stone courthouse in Corydon. When it was very warm, they met out of doors under a big elm tree. Each man wanted to help make the first Indiana constitution the best state constitution in the United States. The first thing they did was to elect a man named Jonathan Jennings president of the constitutional convention.

Jonathan Jennings

Jonathan Jennings had come to the Indiana Territory in 1806, when he was 23 years old. Like many other settlers, he had come down the Ohio River from Pennsylvania. For a while he had lived in Vincennes, where he became a lawyer. Then, he had moved to Clark County where he married.

Jonathan Jennings was a handsome man, with sharp blue eyes and a big, friendly smile. Almost all the settlers who knew the young lawyer liked him. It was not long before the settlers elected Jonathan Jen-

Jonathan Jennings

nings their territorial delegate. The territorial delegate was a man chosen to speak for the territory before the Congress of the United States.

It was not only because he could speak well for the settlers that Jonathan Jennings was elected territorial delegate. He was elected for another reason as well. The young lawyer went to the settlers' farms and talked to them as he helped them with their work. Jonathan Jennings could pitch hay, roll logs and chop down trees, as well as any pioneer. He could play the games the settlers enjoyed. The people liked him for all of these things.

111

Constitution elm at Corydon

The New Constitution

The men at Corydon believed that a state constitution should protect the rights of the people. The constitution:

Allowed every white male who was 21 years or older, and who had lived in Indiana for at least one year, to vote.

Promised that the people could worship in whatever church they pleased.

Granted people freedom of speech and freedom of the press.

Made sure a person charged with a crime had a fair trial by a jury of his fellowmen.

Did not permit one man to own another man as a slave.

Promised the state would set up good schools.

The 43 men at Corydon wrote these ideas into Indiana's first constitution.

Other parts of the new constitution called for a government that would work in three parts. It was to work the same as the government of the United States did.

The Legislature

The first part of Indiana's government would be the legislature. This part would be made up of two groups of men, the Senate and the House of Representatives. These two groups would be called the Legislature, or General Assembly, of Indiana.

The people of the state would elect the men of the legislature. The legislature would meet once a year in the state capital. Later, this part of the constitution was changed so that the General Assembly met only every other year. The men of the Legislature would make new laws that would meet the needs of the state of Indiana.

The Governor

The second part of the government called for one man, the governor, to take charge of what was called the executive part of the government. The governor, like the legislature, would be elected by the people of the state.

The governor was to enforce the laws and take care of the business of the state. He would tell the legislature about the problems of the state and help them solve those problems. The governor could help new laws pass by approving them.

He could stop new laws by vetoing, or disapproving, them. And he had the power to pardon criminals.

The Courts

The third part of Indiana's government was called the judicial (jŏŏ-dĭsh'əl) part. There were three kinds of courts. The highest court would be the state Supreme Court, with three judges. The next highest courts would be the circuit courts, which would work within Indiana's thirteen counties. A third kind of court would work in each township. The judge of such a court was a Justice of the Peace.

The state Supreme Court would judge whether state, city and town laws were fair, according to the constitution. It could also judge criminal cases, if it thought they were important enough.

After 18 days of hard work on Indiana's new constitution, the men at Corydon finished their job. Jonathan Jennings was the first man to sign the constitution.

In August of 1816, an election was held to fill the legislature and the other government jobs. Jonathan Jennings was elected governor.

William Hendricks was elected congressman to speak for the state of Indiana in the United States

House of Representatives. In November of the same year, the legislature elected James Noble and Waller Taylor as members of the United States Senate.

Statehood

Congress soon approved the new constitution and the state government. And on December 11, 1816, after President James Madison gave his approval, the Indiana Territory became the state of Indiana . . . the nineteenth star in the flag of the United States of America.

For the settlers and their elected government, it had been a long wait from the Ordinance of 1787 to the year of statehood.

New Laws for Indiana

When the first legislature of the state of Indiana met in 1816, it made some new laws to take the place of some of the old Indiana Territory laws. For example, men who had broken the law in the Indiana Territory were often whipped instead of sent to jail. That was because Indiana had not had a territorial prison.

The legislature voted for building a large, new state prison. When the prison was built, the whipping post was no longer used.

Other new laws called for new roads to be built, old roads to be fixed, fair elections and better ways to collect taxes.

The Last Indians in Indiana

When Indiana became a state, more than half of her land still belonged to the Indians. The United States government continued making treaties with the Indians to buy their lands, just as Governor Harrison had done. Once the Indians had sold their land to the United States, they had to move west. The government agreed to give the Indians new lands there.

The first large group of Indians to leave Indiana was the Delaware tribe. When they left, in 1820, the central part of Indiana was open for settlers.

The next large Indian group to leave Indiana was the Potawatomi tribe, which lived in northern and western Indiana. One soldier, who saw them leave, said:

"It was sad to see these children of the forest slowly retiring from the home of their childhood. . . . They felt that they were saying goodbye to the hills, valleys and streams of their youth.

"As they looked back, tears fell from the cheeks of the downcast warriors, old men trembled,

The Potowatomi Indians leave their homes.

women wept. They passed along, some on horse back and some on foot and others in wagons. Every now and then one of them would break back to their old camps, saying they would rather die than be banished from their country." The soldier went on to say, "The red man's broken bow had fallen from his hand—his sad heart was bleeding within him."

The United States had to make many treaties with the Potawatomi before they would leave. But when they had gone, much more of Indiana was open to settlers.

The last big Indian tribe to leave Indiana was the Miami tribe, in northeast Indiana. By 1840, the Miami had sold all their land to the United States. In 1846, the Miami were taken by United States soldiers to the new land they had been given in Kansas. The Miami were homesick for their lands in Indiana. During their first winter in Kansas many Miami died from the cold and storms.

By 1846, when the Miami left, all of Indiana was open to settlers. The United States government had solved the Indian problem for the settlers. But the answer to that problem was not a happy one for the Indians. They had felt that Indiana's land was theirs. For many years, they would not even think of selling it.

When one Indian chief was asked to sell his tribe's land, he said, "Sell a country? That is like selling the sky, the winds and the stars!"

Most Indians felt the same way. But the settlers were there, and more would soon come. And they would not turn back.

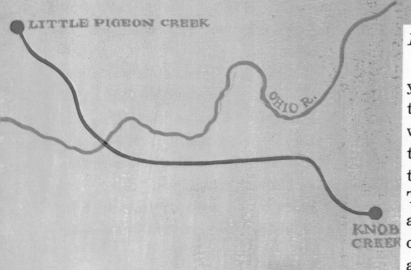

Abraham Lincoln
his hand and pen.
he will be good but
god knows when

13

Abraham Lincoln— The Growing Years

100 Miles to Indiana

It was an exciting day for seven-year-old Abe Lincoln and his sister, Sarah, who was nine. For they were moving. They were leaving their home in Knob Creek, Kentucky, and going into the Indiana Territory. Their father, Tom, had already picked out a quarter section of land there, and had even put up a temporary shelter on it.

116

THE
HOLY BIBLE,
CONTAINING
THE OLD AND NEW
TESTAMENTS:
WITH
ARGUMENTS
OBSERVATIONS

1799

OHIO

Thomas Lincoln
1776~1851

Abraham Lincoln
1809~1865

OHIO R.

KENTUCKY

117

DAVE
KINNEY

Tom Lincoln had his reasons for leaving Kentucky. His land had not been surveyed properly, and now other people were claiming it. Even though Tom Lincoln had paid for his farm and worked hard to improve it, the law said it wasn't his.

That was bad enough. But now there was a fight in their church over slavery. Some people in Kentucky owned slaves. Others, including Tom Lincoln, thought slavery was wrong.

Tom Lincoln was sure he and his family would be much happier in the new area. Pioneers of that time often felt as Tom Lincoln did. If a farm wasn't working out, all a settler had to do was move on. America was a big country, and there was good land to be had further on, if a man wasn't afraid to start all over again someplace else.

The Lincoln family traveled by wagon from Knob Creek as far as the Ohio River. When they reached the Ohio, they took a ferry across. What an exciting sight this was for Abe and Sarah, who had never seen anything bigger than a creek!

The last part of the 100-mile trip from Kentucky to their new home in Pigeon Creek was the hardest. On the other side of the Ohio, the Lincolns still had sixteen miles of thick woods to battle with. Tom Lincoln walked ahead and cut down trees to make a path for the wagon.

Building a New Home

Once the Lincolns reached Pigeon Creek, the whole family helped put up the cabin. Young Abe was only seven, but he knew how to handle an ax. He split thin pieces of wood. Then Abe pushed them between the logs wherever he found an empty space. It was Sarah's job to wet clay and fill in the spaces Abe left.

Like many pioneer cabins, the Lincoln home stood in the unbroken wilderness. And, like other pioneer settlers, Tom Lincoln had to make a clearing in the woods. While he chopped down the big trees, Abe hacked away at the thick undergrowth. This was not unusual. Boys always helped their fathers. Abe also had to keep the woodbox full, clear away the ashes and bring water to the cabin.

When Tom Lincoln furrowed the ground, Abe dropped the seed for corn planting. He and Sarah gathered berries in the spring, and fruit and nuts in the fall. In the spring, too, Abe helped his father tap the maple trees for sugar. Abe loved to sit up late at night, watching the fire under the big kettle. When the sap was boiled down, there would be almost a year's supply of sugar, with plenty of sugar candy for Sarah and Abe.

Most boys went hunting with their fathers, too, but not Abe. He would not hunt. Abe had shot a wild turkey once. When he went to pick it up, he was sickened by the sight. The beautiful bird, so magnificent in life, lay torn and dead. Abe covered his face and wept. It was the last time Abe ever harmed a creature of the woods.

The boys knew Abe was different. Although Abe was only seven when he came to the new state of Indiana, he could read and write. This was something many grownups of that time could not do, including Abe's own father, Tom.

The Joy of Reading

Tom Lincoln couldn't read, but he knew how to tell a story. Sometimes he would tell the children about Daniel Boone. Other times Tom would talk about adventures his own family had with the Indians. When Tom Lincoln spoke, Abe and Sarah could almost see the Indians moving silently through the night.

Nancy Hanks Lincoln could read. She often read to the children from

the Bible. Abe could read from the Bible, too. He and Sarah had gone to school for a while in Kentucky. Often Abe had written his letters down with a piece of charcoal. If nothing else was handy, he used the back of an old wooden shovel.

Abe had a speller, which became a favorite book. At the back of the book were stories, called *Aesop's Fables*. Abe read the fables over and over and never forgot them. For when Abe liked a story, he could repeat it almost word for word.

When Abe was eight years old, his mother's aunt and uncle, the Sparrows, came to live on Tom Lincoln's land. They brought with them a young relative, a boy called Dennis Hanks. One short year later the Sparrows were dead. A terrible disease, the "milk sickness," had taken their lives. The boy, Dennis Hanks, came to live with the Lincolns.

Abe Loses His Mother

The "milk sickness" spread, and soon Tom Lincoln was sadly making coffins for his neighbors. All through these troubled times, Nancy Hanks Lincoln went to help her family and friends. And then Nancy herself became sick. A week later, Tom Lincoln was making another coffin, and young Abe, blinded by tears, was helping.

Life in the wilderness was always hard and lonely. But never had it been so hard and so lonely as it was now, with the loving voice of the wife and mother silent forever.

Abe and Sarah grew closer together in their sorrow. Now it was eleven-year-old Sarah who had to be the woman of the house. She tried to take her mother's place. As best she could, she cooked and cleaned and sewed. But at night, the sad and weary little girl sat by the fire and cried for her mother.

The unhappy little boy didn't know what to do. He thought that a pet might cheer Sarah up. So he caught a baby raccoon and a turtle and brought them to her. In this way, more than a year passed. But a pioneer family could not go on without a woman to run the house.

A New Mother for the Lincoln Family

A woman Tom had known in Kentucky, Sarah Bush Johnston, was a widow now. Tom felt certain that Sarah Johnston would be a good mother for his children. He went back to Kentucky to ask her to be his wife.

The new Mrs. Lincoln brought a household of furniture, three children and a heart full of love. Someone said, "She took the children and mixed them up together like hasty pudding," and loved them all the same.

She had also brought treasures that made Abe open his eyes in wonder—books! One was *Robinson Crusoe*. Another was *The Arabian Nights*. Dennis Hanks thought *The Arabian Nights* was "a pack of lies." Abe Lincoln just laughed and said, "Yes. But they are mighty fine lies!"

121

Abraham gave Sarah a baby raccoon and a turtle.

Abe would lie on his stomach at night in front of the fire and read the stories out loud. Every once in a while, he would stop reading and start to laugh. When Abe laughed, everyone else laughed, too.

Abe and Sarah were going to school again, for there was a new schoolhouse in Pigeon Creek. School only lasted for a short time, but Mrs. Lincoln made sure all the Lincoln children went. She thought reading, writing and arithmetic were important, especially for Abe.

Abe read more and remembered more than anybody she could think of. If Abe heard that a neighbor had a book, he would walk miles to borrow it.

How Abe Had Fun

Abe liked to read, but he was as full of mischief as most boys his age. He was the tallest, strongest boy in Pigeon Creek. He liked to run and jump and wrestle. And fun was where he found it!

Once he saw a cow standing at the garden gate. Abe jumped on her back, dug his bare feet into her side, and made that cow go galloping down the road, much to the cow's surprise. And while he rode her, Abe shouted and sang at the top of his voice, shaking his hat wildly in the air. What a funny sight that must have been, the tall, skinny boy riding a cow down a dirt road!

The Lincolns, like most pioneer families, went to church regularly. Abe listened carefully to the preacher's sermons. When they came home, Abe would jump up on the stump of a tree. Then he would repeat the sermon, waving his arms and making faces just like the preacher. Other times he would make speeches. After a while, Tom had to make Abe stop. For Abe was so interesting, everyone sat and listened to him instead of attending to their chores!

Learning About America

Soon Tom Lincoln was asked to build a new church in Pigeon Creek. Since he was a fine carpenter he did all the woodwork inside the church.

When the church was finished, Abe took over the job of keeping the church clean. He also made sure there was a supply of wood for the fire and plenty of candles were on hand.

Meanwhile, Abe had discovered two books that taught him something about his country, and two Americans who had helped make his country great. The first was a

Abe dug his heels in and rode the cow home.

book written by Benjamin Franklin, in which he told the story of his life. The second was about George Washington. Abe began to understand the history of the land he lived in, and the men who had fought to make it free.

How Abe Worked

By the time Abe was fifteen, he had almost reached his full growth of six feet four inches. People teased Abe about his long arms and legs. But they admired his strength.

He could handle an ax as if it were part of his hand. A friend said, "If you heard him felling trees in a clearing, you would say there were three men at work, the way the trees fell." There was no doubt in anyone's mind that Abe Lincoln was a master woodsman.

Once Abe reached the age of sixteen, he was finished with school. Now it was time for him to get a regular job. His father thought Abe might like to become a carpenter, but Abe didn't much like the idea of woodworking. And he didn't care for farming, either.

Abe hired himself out to the neighbors, some of whom paid him 25¢ for a full day's work. Then he got a job he really enjoyed. He was asked to help run a ferry across Anderson River. Abe was delighted.

While Abe ferried people from one side of the river to the other, he helped pass the time by telling them stories. Soon the children of the settlements on both sides of the river waited at the landings to hear Abe talk. Abe was getting paid 6½¢ round trip to take people back and forth, but the storytelling was free!

Abe had built a small rowboat, which he kept at the landing. One day two men asked Abe if he would row them out to the middle of the river, where they could catch a steamer. Abe was glad to do it, and found himself rewarded with two silver dollars as payment! Abe had never had so much money at one time in his life!

Working at the river opened a whole new world for Abe. More people than Abe had ever seen in his life traveled up and down the river.

It was while Abe was working at the river that his life was filled with sorrow again. His sister, Sarah, who had watched over him and cared for him, died. She was twenty-one years old. When Abe was told, he sat down and put his face in his hands. Tears ran down through his fingers, and his body shook with great sobs. The friend and compan-ion of his growing years was gone.

A few months later, Abe was asked by a storekeeper, James Gentry, if he would help Gentry's son take a flatboat to New Orleans. Abe was delighted at the idea of going to this strange and wonderful city at the mouth of the Mississippi River. He had heard many stories about New Orleans.

The Trip to New Orleans

It was a long and dangerous trip for a boy of nineteen. From Indiana to New Orleans, Allen Gentry and Abe Lincoln traveled more than 1,000 miles. Navigating the flatboat was difficult work, for Abe had to watch out for rocks and sunken trees in the river. And river pirates might try to seize their cargo.

When Abe left on the trip to New Orleans, he was nineteen. He was twenty when he came back. The journey, round trip, had taken al-most a year.

In New Orleans, Abe saw many things that excited and interested him. And it was here that he had his first sight of slaves being sold on the auction block. The sale of human beings was something Abe never forgot. He had been brought up in a family that was against slavery.

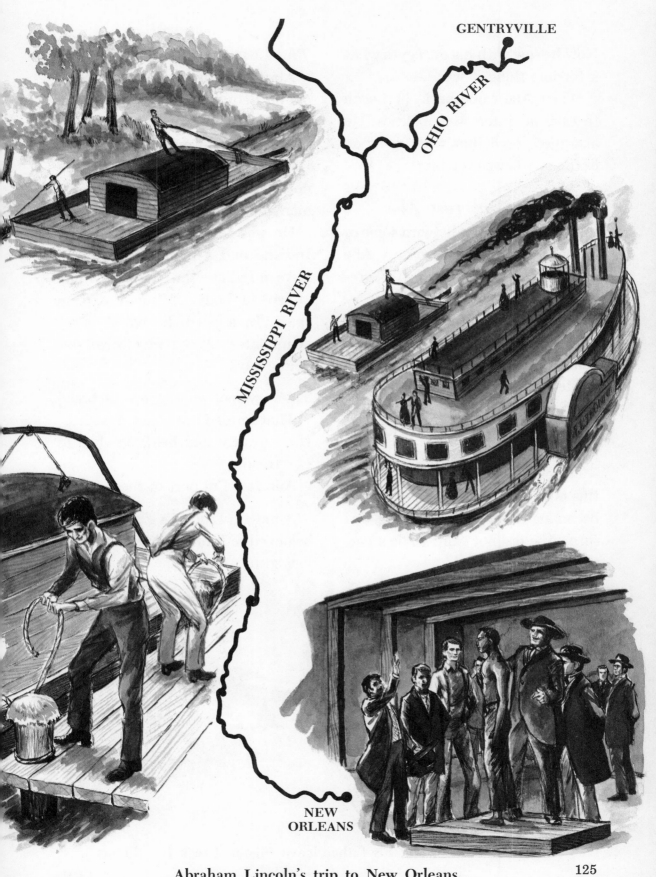

GENTRYVILLE

OHIO RIVER

MISSISSIPPI RIVER

NEW ORLEANS

Abraham Lincoln's trip to New Orleans.

125

Now he saw with his own eyes what a terrible thing it was.

When Abe came back, he began to take an interest in politics. He also discovered that what went on in the courts was exciting.

New Ideas Interest Abe

Abe became friendly with some of the lawyers. One of them gave Abe a lawbook to read. It was *The Revised Laws of Indiana* (1824).

In this book, Abe read for the first time the Declaration of Independence, the Constitution of the United States, the Constitution of the State of Indiana, and the History of the Territory and State of Indiana.

No one knows if the reading of this book first gave Abe the idea of becoming a lawyer. One thing was sure: Abe did not want to be a carpenter or a farmer.

The Lincolns Leave Indiana

Abraham Lincoln was 21 years old on February 12, 1830. It was in this year that once again Tom Lincoln decided to move, this time to Illinois. Though Abe moved to Illinois with his father, he was now a man and soon went his own way.

He was seven when he came to Indiana and a man when he left. Here in Indiana the pioneer boy had grown—in body, in mind and in spirit. In a poem he wrote many years later, Abe remembered his young days:

The very spot where grew the bread
    That formed my bones, I see.
How strange, old field, on thee to
    tread
    And feel I'm part of thee!

Abraham Lincoln's growing years belonged to Indiana. And his life belonged to America.

126   Abraham Lincoln and his father leave Pigeon Creek for Illinois.

Harmonie street scene

14

Indiana—A Testing Ground for New Ideas

A Land of New Ideas

Early America was a place where men wanted to build a strong, free nation for themselves, and for the people who would come after them. In those early years, there were many puzzling questions about how to make democracy work. And there were many different ideas about how to make democracy work. Indiana was one testing ground for some of these different ideas.

New Ideas in Living

In 1804, a group of German immigrants had come to America, looking for religious freedom. They had settled in Pennsylvania, not far from Pittsburgh. They had done well there, but they wanted a location close to a river, and one with a better climate. The leader of this group of nearly a thousand people was Father George Rapp. Father Rapp chose a place on the Wabash River in the Indiana Territory.

Father Rapp believed that people could live in perfect harmony. To do this, they had to live together as complete equals. They had to share all their property equally. They had to share all work equally. Most of all, they had to believe strongly in the religion of Father Rapp.

The Rappites, as they were called, had tried to set up their own community in Germany. But this kind of special group was not liked in Germany. So the Rappites fled to America.

Unlike most other pioneers, the Rappites saw no reason to build a better world for the people who would come after them. They believed the world would end during their lifetimes.

They did not want to bring children into a world that would soon end. Their aims in life called for hard work and brotherly love. Father Rapp, who was a strong leader and a kind man, made sure that each Rappite did his share of the work.

The Rappites called their Indiana settlement *Harmonie*. By the year 1816, when Indiana became a state, the community was thriving. The Rappites kept many kinds of farm animals. They grew many different crops. Whatever they needed for day-to-day use, such as clothes and tools, they also made themselves. They lived almost completely within their own settlement.

The Rappites were also known for their love of music. Almost everyone in the community could play an instrument. And they loved to sing. They sang even while they worked.

The Rappites were fond of flowers, too, and flowers were grown everywhere. Cut flowers were found in all the Rappite buildings.

In 1825, the Rappites left Harmonie. They moved to a new location in Pennsylvania. They left behind a beautiful community in the Indiana wilderness.

New Harmony

After the Rappites left, Harmonie was taken over by a man named Robert Owen. Robert Owen had become famous in Scotland for the way he ran his cotton mills.

In most parts of Britain and Europe at that time, factory workers got little pay for their work, and they lived in shacks, often without even enough to eat. Robert Owen was a different kind of employer. He shortened working hours and gave his workers more pay. He even built schools and libraries for them.

Robert Owen believed in the equality of all men. He believed that every man should have the right to live without fear and without want. He would have liked to see a whole country built on this idea.

He therefore bought the settlement of Harmonie from the Rappites and invited all who were interested in his idea to come and live there. Robert Owen had no trouble finding followers. Soon his town, renamed New Harmony, was filled with more than a thousand people.

Many sincere, hard-working men and women came to New Harmony. But others came who were not interested in anything but themselves. The sincere people hoped to see Robert Owen's dream come true. The others were just looking for an easy life.

Robert Owen knew that one of the keys to a great society was

Robert Owen welcomes teachers to New Harmony.

education. He brought many fine teachers to New Harmony. There were schools for grownups as well as for the children. Even children as young as two years went to school. New Harmony is remembered as the birthplace of the kindergarten.

The schools of New Harmony, along with its large library and its fine artists and scholars, made the town famous.

But in spite of all the good things about Robert Owen's settlement, it failed. The people who lived in New Harmony could not work as well as the Rappites had. Many of them could not do the jobs they were supposed to do. Others simply did as little work as possible.

Although Robert Owen's plan failed, the town of New Harmony continued on its own. For many years, New Harmony was the home of David Dale Owen, Robert Owen's son. David Owen was a fine scientist and Indiana's first state geologist. He made New Harmony the center of geological study in the Midwest for many years.

On August 22, 1965, New Harmony was made a national historic landmark.

The Problem of Slavery

People of early America were troubled with many problems. One of the problems that divided the country was slavery. The whole southern part of America was built on slavery. Negro slaves were used to work the farms. Without slaves, the people of the south would have had a hard time working the land.

In the north, many people were against slavery. They said it was wrong for one man to own another. They wanted the slaves to be set free.

Indiana was caught between those who wanted slavery and those who did not. In the southern part of Indiana, where many of the settlers had come from slave states, slavery was looked upon as a normal way of life. But in the northern part of Indiana, many looked upon slavery as an evil thing. Many religious groups, such as the Methodists and the Quakers, spoke out strongly against the idea of slaveholding. The argument between those who had different ideas about slavery grew stronger and more violent.

The Runaway Slave

At last people in the north began to help slaves who had run away from their owners. They had to do this in secret, for it was against the law to help a runaway slave. But these people felt the law was wrong. The stories the runaway slaves told made the people of the north hate slavery more than ever.

One of the stories they heard was from a slave named Rachel, who had lived in Kentucky with her husband and children. Not all slave owners were harsh. Rachel's owners were kind people. But after a while, the owners sold Rachel's husband. They thought nothing of breaking up the family, for kind as they were, they still thought of their slaves as they did their cattle or horses or any of their possessions.

Rachel grieved for her husband, but soon she had even worse trouble. Her owner died, and Rachel was sold to a man who had a plantation in Mississippi. Before this, Rachel had always worked in the kitchen. Now suddenly, she was put to work in the fields. She did not know what to do in the fields, and her new owner whipped her because he did not like the way she worked.

It was not long before Rachel ran away. It took her four months to get back to Kentucky, for she could only walk at night. Once again, her luck ran out. Her owner found her.

Rachel only could travel at night.

He put handcuffs on her hands. On her feet, he put an iron chain and ball. Rachel could hardly move. But she felt she had to be free.

One night she crept out of the wagon that was taking her back south. She hid behind some large rocks.

Night after night she crawled, until she reached the Ohio River. Somehow, she made her way across the Ohio into Indiana.

Kind people brought her to the home of a man called Levi Coffin. Here she stayed six months, until she was well enough to travel on to freedom in Canada.

Levi Coffin and the "Underground Railroad"

Levi Coffin, the Indiana Quaker who helped her, was among those who worked hardest to help the slaves. He lived in Newport, now Fountain City, Indiana, where he had a large house. From this house he ran what came to be known as the Underground Railroad.

The Underground Railroad was not a railroad at all. It was made up of a group of people. They were scattered over Indiana, Ohio and Kentucky. These people all had one idea, to help runaway slaves escape to free territory in Canada.

131

Levi Coffin helps runaway slaves.

The people of the Underground Railroad always talked about themselves in a kind of code. Calling it a "railroad" was of course a code in itself. Every member at a particular town was called an "agent," and those who took slaves from one "station" to another were called "conductors."

In Indiana, the railroad had stations in many important towns. Madison, Indianapolis, Richmond and Evansville were a few of the main stations for the underground.

Levi Coffin ran the Underground Railroad from Indiana for twenty years, from 1827 to 1847. In that time, it is believed he helped more than 2,000 slaves escape.

Levi Coffin moved to Cincinnati, Ohio, in 1847, and continued his Underground Railroad until the Civil War began.

The Greatest Test

The time before the Civil War was a time of testing ideas. Harmonie and New Harmony were tests to see if people could live together in harmony and equality. The Underground Railroad was a test to see if the idea of freedom for all the people was stronger than the idea that freedom was just for some of the people. This idea was put to its greatest test when the people of the south and the people of the north went to war in the year 1861.

CHAPTER 15—HOW SLAVERY CAME TO AMERICA

8000 B.C. to 1400 A.D. — Slavery is as old as the history of man. Men and women taken prisoners after a battle were made slaves.

4000 B.C. to 1500 A.D. — In many countries, in Europe, Asia and Africa, a man who owed money he could not pay back, became a slave.

1441 — Slave trade in Europe began when Portuguese brought back from Africa 12 Negro men, women and children to Portugal.

1500 to 1800 — Between 17 million and 23 million people were taken from Africa to be sold as slaves.

1619 — Dutch ship brings 20 Negroes to Jamestown. The beginning of slavery in America.

1807 — England abolished slave trade.

1808 — United States abolished slave trade.

1833 — England abolished slavery.

15

How Slavery Came To America

The History of Slavery

Slavery is almost as old as the history of man. Exactly how and why slavery began is not known. Perhaps it started when the first people to conquer another people decided to let their prisoners live as slaves instead of killing them. Even the Bible mentions slavery.

In the ancient times of Greece and Rome, men and women taken prisoners after a battle were made slaves. This was one way that people became slaves, but there were other ways, too.

For example, it was not unusual in Greece or Rome, for a man to become a slave if he borrowed money and could not pay it back. He became the slave of the man to whom he owed the money. Often, a man sold a daughter, if he needed money. The daughter would then become a slave to the man she was sold to. And, of course, children born to slaves were slaves as well.

There was slavery among the people in Africa, too. As in Europe and Asia, a man became a slave if he owed money, or if he was captured in battle. But he also became a slave if he committed a crime. Instead of going to prison, he was sent to work as a slave in the home of the person he wronged.

In Greece and in Rome, slaves were allowed to save money to buy their freedom. But in most countries, the only way a slave could be a free man was if his master set him free.

How Slavery Began In America

To understand how slavery began in America, it is necessary to go back to the time when the Portuguese began to explore the African coast. Prince Henry of Portugal wanted gold, and he sent ships to Africa to look for it. The Portuguese did not find gold, but when they returned to Portugal in 1441 they brought back about twelve Negro men, women and children. This was the beginning of slavery in Europe. The Portuguese sold more and more Negroes in Portugal and then in Spain.

When the other countries, such as Spain, England, France, and Holland, saw how much money could be made in slave trading, they set up slave trading posts in Africa, too.

Slaves captive in Africa

When the New World was discovered, Englishmen and Spaniards brought slaves and sold them to the colonists. In the three hundred years between the sixteenth and nineteenth centuries, more than 20 million men and women were taken from Africa and sold as slaves.

At first, slave traders bought Negro slaves from African chiefs. These Negro slaves had usually been taken as prisoners in tribal wars. But then European nations became greedy for more and more slaves. It was then they began to kidnap African men and women from their villages.

The Slave Trade

In colonial days in America there was a great deal of hard work to be done and there were not enough people to do it. It was hard to get workmen for farms and plantations, for most people wanted to own their own farms and work for themselves.

American shipowners, who had sailed the seas to bring back goods from other countries now saw that fortunes could be made by bringing slaves from Africa to America. These shipowners were called slave traders.

The slave traders sold the Negroes in both northern and southern colonies. But it soon became clear

135

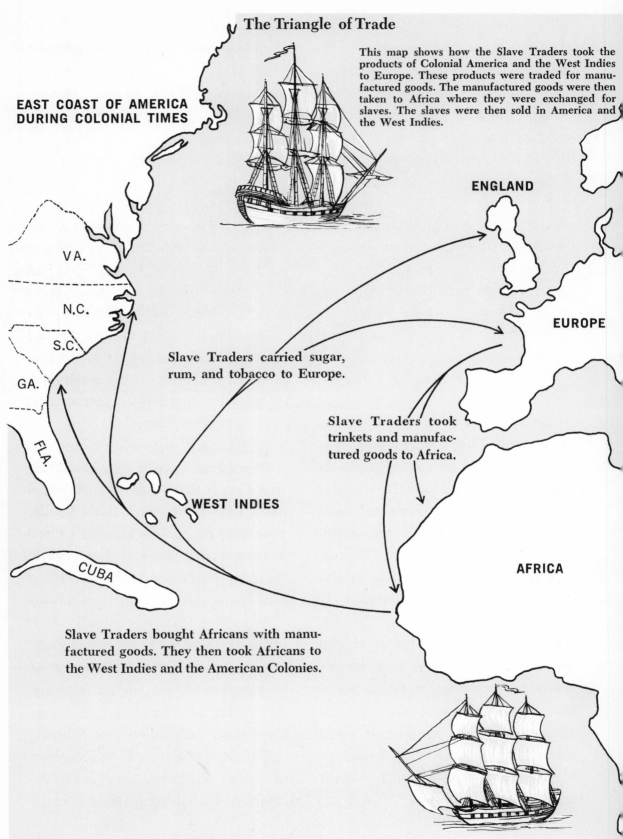

The Triangle of Trade

This map shows how the Slave Traders took the products of Colonial America and the West Indies to Europe. These products were traded for manufactured goods. The manufactured goods were then taken to Africa where they were exchanged for slaves. The slaves were then sold in America and the West Indies.

EAST COAST OF AMERICA DURING COLONIAL TIMES

VA.

N.C.

S.C.

GA.

FLA.

ENGLAND

EUROPE

Slave Traders carried sugar, rum, and tobacco to Europe.

Slave Traders took trinkets and manufactured goods to Africa.

WEST INDIES

CUBA

AFRICA

Slave Traders bought Africans with manufactured goods. They then took Africans to the West Indies and the American Colonies.

that slavery was not profitable in the North. Although there was plenty of field work in the summer, in the long winter months the slaves had nothing to do. The northern owners felt it cost too much to care for slaves when they were not working.

For a time it seemed likely that slavery might disappear in the South. But then the growing of cotton became important, and slaves became necessary to plantation owners. The price of slaves went up. In the 1850's, a strong field worker might cost $1,500.

Slave Trading Is Abolished

Although the idea of slavery was a very old one, there had always been people who thought slavery was evil. In England, the Quakers were so horrified by slavery that they fought long and hard against slave trading.

Finally, in 1772, a law was passed in England saying the moment a slave set foot on English soil, he was free. In 1807, England abolished the slave trade. In 1808, the United States abolished the slave trade,

too. But greedy men, who did not wish to give up this profitable trade, continued to bring slaves to America even though it was against the law.

By this time, many people in the United States, especially in the North, decided that they did not like the idea of slavery. Feelings ran high among those who were against it, and those who were for it. Hoosiers themselves did not all agree. Some felt the North should mind its own business and leave slavery to the South. Others thought it wrong and wanted to keep it from spreading. A smaller but growing number wanted to end it everywhere.

In England, in 1833, a law was passed abolishing slavery. The slaves were freed, and the government paid all the slave owners to make up the money they lost. But in the United States, things were different. The South had been built on the work of slaves. The Southerners felt they could not get along without slaves now. And there was too much anger on both sides for the matter to be settled peacefully.

1854 — The Anti-slavery party (Republican party) is formed.

November, 1860 — Abraham Lincoln is elected president. Indiana gives Lincoln 25,000 more votes than it gives to any other candidate.

December 20, 1860 — South Carolina, the first state to secede, leaves the Union.

April 12, 1861 — The Civil War begins when Southern cannon fire on Fort Sumter.

July 21, 1861 — The first battle of Bull Run is fought.

April 6-7, 1862 — The Battle of Shiloh is fought.

January 1, 1863 — Abraham Lincoln issues the Emancipation Proclamation.

July 1-3, 1863 — The Battle of Gettysburg is fought.

July 8-13, 1863 — Morgan's Raiders invade Indiana.

April 9, 1865 — General Robert E. Lee surrenders to General Ulysses S. Grant.

1861-1865 — Indiana raised over 200,000 soldiers for the North. More than 24,000 of Indiana's soldiers died in the Civil War.

16

Indiana and the Civil War

Reasons for the Civil War

War, like slavery, goes back into ancient times. Nations have fought other nations for many reasons. And at times, people within a country have fought one another, too. This kind of war, where people in the same country find themselves on opposite sides of a fight, is called a civil war.

Civil wars have been fought in England, in Russia, in Spain and in China. In the United States, too, Americans fought Americans for four long years in a terrible and bitter Civil War.

Many things led up to this war. The people of the North believed in a strong national government. Southerners wanted the state governments to be stronger than the national government.

Southern states thought they should be allowed to leave the United States and form their own government, if they wanted to do so. Northern states did not believe the country should be divided.

Most of all, the North and South could not come to an agreement on the question of slavery.

The Republican Party

In 1854, a new anti-slavery party was formed. It was called the Republican Party. In 1860, the Republicans chose Abraham Lincoln to be their candidate for president. Lincoln was popular with Hoosiers, who remembered that he had grown up in Indiana. He won the election over three other candidates in a close race. Indiana gave Abraham Lincoln 25,000 more votes than any other candidate.

Angry southerners said that they could not remain in the Union if the Republican Party won the election. When Abraham Lincoln became the President of the United States, the southerners kept their word. First South Carolina, and then other southern states, left the Union. A new southern government was formed, with its own constitution, and its own president. Jefferson Davis of Mississippi was the president of the southern government.

The Civil War Starts

Abraham Lincoln did not believe the South had any right to leave the

Union. He felt that the important thing was to keep the United States together. But the new southern government did not want to stay in the Union.

In April, 1861, southerners fired on the flag flying over Fort Sumter at Charleston, South Carolina. The following day, the Union soldiers in Fort Sumter surrendered. The Civil War had begun.

Though Hoosiers before the war had been both for and against slavery, they now supported President Lincoln.

Oliver P. Morton

One of the Indiana leaders in the new Republican Party was a man named Oliver P. Morton. Oliver P. Morton, who was born at Centerville, Indiana, was the first native Hoosier to become governor. Morton believed strongly that the Union must be saved. As governor, he did everything he could to help Lincoln and the war effort.

Governor Morton was a good friend to the soldiers. He was never too busy to go to the railroad station and say good-by when the troop trains left Indianapolis for the South. Medicine, food and extra clothing were supplied to the soldiers through organizations set up by Governor Morton. When an unfriendly legislature would not give him enough money for the army's needs, he borrowed the money himself and bought supplies for Hoosier soldiers. His enemies called him a tyrant and a dictator. His friends said he was a patriot, who did what had to be done.

The Civil War brought change and suffering to Indiana, as it did to the nation. Life was hard for the families the soldiers left behind. Women and children had to run the farms. With the men gone to fight in the war, women began to do work they had never done before. They became clerks in stores, workers in factories, teachers and nurses.

Morgan's Raiders

Most of the fighting in the Civil War was done in the South. But the war came to Indiana in July, 1863, when a southern general, John Morgan, invaded Indiana with about 2,400 southern horse soldiers. He and his men seized two river steamers, then crossed the Ohio River into Indiana near Mauckport.

A handful of Hoosiers at the river tried to stop them with one cannon but they were swept aside. The Hoosiers tried again to stop Morgan just south of Corydon. About 400

Some of Morgan's Raiders stole ice skates, sleigh bells and bird cage with three canaries.

home guards held off Morgan's men on a wooded ridge for several hours. Even the southern officers said the Hoosiers fought bravely, but they were too few to stop Morgan.

Morgan's soldiers moved quickly across southeastern Indiana. The Confederates (kən-fĕd′ər-ĭts), as they were called, moved so fast they wore out their horses. When they needed fresh horses, the raiders took them from farms they passed. And they complained later that "they rode into Indiana on Kentucky thoroughbreds and rode out on Hoosier plough-horses!"

Morgan told millowners to pay him money or have their mills burned. His men plundered stores and houses as they went. They stole whatever caught their eye.

One of Morgan's raiders wrote later: "The weather was intensely warm—the hot July sun burned the earth to powder, and we were breathing superheated dust—yet one man rode for three days with seven pairs of skates slung about his neck; another loaded himself with sleigh-bells. . . . another raider carried away a birdcage containing three canaries . . ."

Salem, Vienna and Versailles fell into the hands of Morgan and his men, and Vernon was threatened. At Dupont, the raiders stole 2,000

"You sure are purty, Ma'm, when you're in a temper," he said admiringly.

hams from a meat-packer named Mayfield. Each Confederate had his own ham for breakfast. One of Mayfield's daughters gave the southerners a tongue lashing for their piggish thievery. The raiders paid no attention, except for one young man who looked at the angry girl and smiled. "You sure are purty, Ma'm, when you're in a temper," he said admiringly. "After we lick you Yanks, I'll come back and marry you." The Confederates did not lick the Yanks, but the young southern soldier kept his word. He came back and married the girl!

Morgan's raiders crossed into Ohio at the town of Harrison. Although they had been on Indiana soil only five days, they had done a great deal of damage, and Hoosiers were certainly glad to see them go.

End of the Civil War

The war ended on April 9, 1865 when the southern general Robert E. Lee surrendered to the northern general Ulysses S. Grant. People everywhere were grateful the war was over at last. But six short days later, the nation was made sad again. President Lincoln was murdered. Hoosiers especially felt the loss of their President. They had last seen him when he was on his way to Washington. As his train crossed Indiana, people had waved in friendly greeting, and he had waved back.

In Indianapolis, Mr. Lincoln had ridden in a parade with Governor Morton and the mayor of Indianapolis. And Mr. Lincoln had made a speech from the balcony of the Bates House. Now the funeral train took Abraham Lincoln back to Illinois to be buried. But it stopped in Indianapolis on April 20, so weeping Hoosiers could come and say their last farewells to a man who now "belonged to the ages." Lincoln saved the union and ended slavery.

Indiana's record in the Civil War was a proud one. Money and men had been provided generously. Millions of dollars had been spent for uniforms and guns.

Hoosiers had fought bravely wherever they had been sent during the war. Indiana had raised over 200,000 soldiers to fight for the North.

More than 24,000 of these soldiers died in the war. No northern state did more to save and keep the Union together.

The Lincoln funeral train stopped at Indianapolis.

143

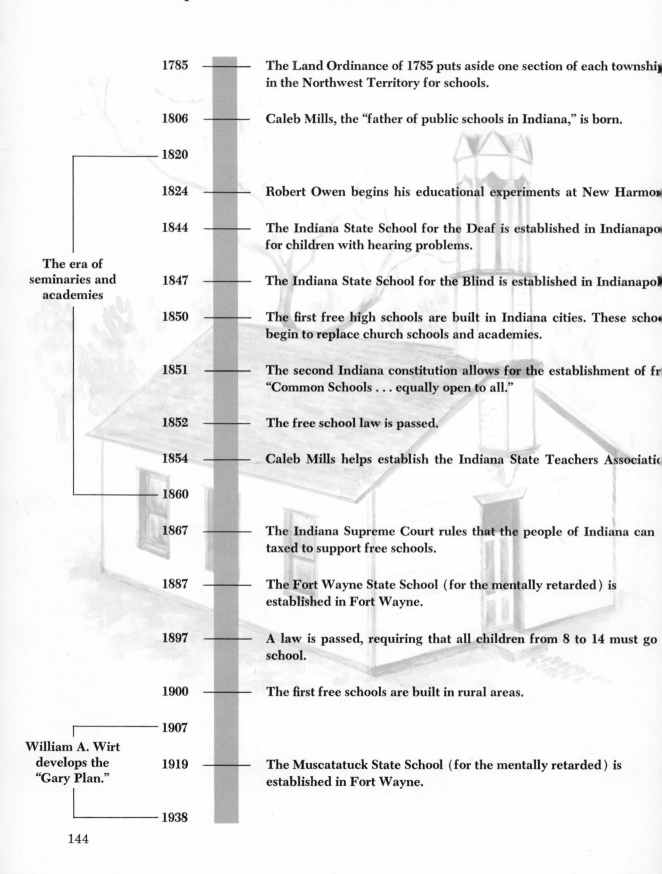

1785	The Land Ordinance of 1785 puts aside one section of each township in the Northwest Territory for schools.
1806	Caleb Mills, the "father of public schools in Indiana," is born.
1820	
1824	Robert Owen begins his educational experiments at New Harmony.
1844	The Indiana State School for the Deaf is established in Indianapolis for children with hearing problems.
1847	The Indiana State School for the Blind is established in Indianapolis.
1850	The first free high schools are built in Indiana cities. These schools begin to replace church schools and academies.
1851	The second Indiana constitution allows for the establishment of free "Common Schools . . . equally open to all."
1852	The free school law is passed.
1854	Caleb Mills helps establish the Indiana State Teachers Association.
1860	
1867	The Indiana Supreme Court rules that the people of Indiana can be taxed to support free schools.
1887	The Fort Wayne State School (for the mentally retarded) is established in Fort Wayne.
1897	A law is passed, requiring that all children from 8 to 14 must go to school.
1900	The first free schools are built in rural areas.
1907	
1919	The Muscatatuck State School (for the mentally retarded) is established in Fort Wayne.
1938	

The era of seminaries and academies

William A. Wirt develops the "Gary Plan."

17

Good Schools Build
A Better Indiana

The Fight for
Free Public Schools

After the Civil War, the nation, and Indiana, began to make plans again, to build a free and strong country. A good way to build for the future was through education.

At one time, before the Civil War, many citizens of Indiana had wanted to set up a free public school system. In the constitution of 1850, the government made it the duty of the legislature to provide free schools in Indiana. Money to run the schools was to be raised by taxes. Each town and city was to tax the people. But there were many people who did not understand how important public schools were. They did not want to pay taxes to run the schools. These people took their arguments to the Supreme Court of Indiana. The Supreme Court decided that the people could not be taxed against their will.

In 1867, the government of the state once more set up a plan for free public schools. And again the government said citizens could be taxed for money to run the schools.

As before, some people did not want to pay taxes to run schools. But this time there were fewer people who were against the idea. But they, too, took their arguments to the Supreme Court. This time, however, the Supreme Court said that since most of the citizens wanted a public school system, it was only right that they should have it. So Indiana got its first public schools.

Then and Now In
Indiana Schools

In early days, children did not have to go to school. Parents often kept children home to do chores. Those who did go usually attended school for only two or three months out of the year. Today, of course, all children must go to school, for everyone realizes the importance of education. And most schools are open eight, nine or ten months during the year.

Back in pioneer times, it was felt a child had enough education if he learned to read and write and do a little arithmetic. Modern schools teach many different subjects, and new ideas are always being brought into the classroom. For example, it was in Gary, Indiana, that children first worked in school libraries, woodshops, kitchens and gyms. In the woodshops, the children learned such things as carpentry, printing and other trades. Soon other schools started to follow Gary's lead.

There was a great change in choosing teachers for schools, too. In pioneer days, a teacher did not need any special training. Often a teacher did not know much more than his pupils. Today's teachers must study long and hard before they come before a class. And many teachers continue to go to special schools in the summer months to keep up with new ideas in education.

Even school buildings changed. It is a long way from the one-room log cabin and the hard wooden benches to today's modern glass and brick buildings, with their big, bright and pleasant classrooms.

As transportation became faster and better, and as more and more children went to school, a movement began to consolidate the schools. This meant that instead of having many small schools, fewer but bigger buildings were put up. And children from a wider area were brought by bus to attend the same school. This was true of high schools as well as elementary schools.

Going to High School

In pioneer times, if a child wanted to go on to high school, he had to attend either a church school, called a parochial (pə-rō′kĭ-əl) school, or a privately run school. There were no free high schools until the 1850's, and then they were built only in the cities. It was not until the 1900's that high schools began to appear in farm areas.

When free high schools were built, they soon replaced most of the private and church-run schools. But there are still many private and parochial schools.

Universities of the Churches and the State

Before the Civil War, the churches in Indiana grew large and strong. Many churches started schools to help develop better education in Indiana.

Soon, these church colleges were all over the state. Although the colleges and universities were run by different churches, they were open to almost anyone who wanted to attend.

Of course, the state, as well as the churches, began to build universities. As far back as 1806 there had

Colless and Universities of Indiana

been a territorial university at Vincennes, called the Vincennes University. Then Indiana University opened its doors in 1824 in Bloomington, and Purdue University, at Lafayette, opened in 1869. In addition to all these schools, several teachers' colleges were started by the state in the late 1800's and early 1900's.

Going to College

At one time very few students went on to a higher education. Up to the 1850's, women were not even allowed to enter most of the colleges, for it was not thought important in those days for girls and women to have a good education.

Today, more and more students go on to college, whether they choose state universities, church universities or private colleges. Often, students may go to colleges in other states. And students from other states come to study at the fine colleges in Indiana. Many students from other countries come to Indi-

ana's colleges and universities, too. People from such far-off places as India and Nigeria are often found on the campus at Indiana University, for example.

Special Schools

Children with special problems have not been forgotten by the state. In addition to its regular schools, the state of Indiana built or improved special schools, too. The Deaf School in Indianapolis, built in 1844, is for children with hearing problems. A school for the blind, started in 1847 in Indianapolis, is for children with sight problems. Both these schools were greatly improved after the Civil War.

After the Civil War, schools were built for retarded children and for delinquent children. The state of Indiana was interested in, and cared for, all of its children. To build a strong, united nation, people have to be educated. Indiana schools are ready to do their share.

Students come from all over the world to study at Indiana colleges and universities.

Chapter 18 . . . Invention and Industry Change Indiana

11 — The first steamboat used in the west, the "New Orleans," steams down the Ohio River.

19 — The steamboat "United States" is built at Jeffersonville.

47 — The Indianapolis-Madison railroad is completed.

50 — Reapers, corn planters, mowers and hay balers become valuable tools of Indiana farmers.

52 — The Studebaker brothers begin to manufacture wagons in South Bend.

68 — James Oliver invents the chilled plow; ten years later, he begins to manufacture it in South Bend.

70 — Indiana limestone becomes known around the world as a fine building material. The manufacture of plate glass begins at New Albany.

80 — Electricity is used for public outdoor lighting in Wabash.

85 — Indiana's first electric street car makes its first run in South Bend.

86 — The Indiana natural gas boom begins in Grant, Howard, Tipton, Hamilton, Madison and Delaware counties.

88 — The Ball brothers open a glass plant in Muncie.

94 — Elwood Haynes builds a "horseless carriage" at Kokomo.

96 — Interurban service begins between Anderson and Alexandria.

06 — The production of steel begins at Gary.

17 — Strip coal mining becomes important in Indiana.

149

Early Craftsmen

Wagon making

Utensil repair

Furniture making

Iron work

Quilt making

Boot making

18

Industry and Invention Change Indiana

The Village Craftsman

The early settler was more than just a farmer. In his own way, he was a trader and a small manufacturer, as well. Clothing, quilts, candles and soap, for example, were just a few of the things the women made. Furniture, such as beds, tables, chairs and cupboards, and many of the farm implements, were made by the men. It was almost like having a small factory in the home.

Not every pioneer was a good farmer. Often a man found that he did not like farming at all. If he had a special skill, he usually gave up farming and became a craftsman. Before long, a number of craftsmen opened small shops in the villages. Then pioneers could buy, rather than make at home, such things as shoes and hats and harnesses.

Of course no village was complete without the blacksmith, for the village blacksmith did more than just shoe horses. He made hoes and axes and hammers, as well as such things as pots and pans and butcher knives. He often put blades in pocket knives. And it was not unusual for a blacksmith to make wagons, too.

With more and more craftsmen setting up shop, it was not surprising that the making of certain products soon moved out of the home into the new and growing small factories. When this happened, new ways of producing products began to take the place of the old ways.

The First Industries

The early manufacturer and factory owner depended on the farmer in two ways. He needed the farmer's crops. And in turn, he had to sell his products to the farmer.

Grist mills made an early appearance, becoming Indiana's first real industry. Millers bought corn and wheat from the farmers. The corn was ground into meal. The wheat was ground into flour. As transportation improved, the mills were able to ship the meal and flour to the large cities in the east.

Other industries grew as farmers began to take more interest in raising hogs. Pork packing, for many years, was one of Indiana's most important industries. Madison, the

Driving hogs through the streets

"Porkopolis" (pôr-kŏp′ə-lĭs) of the Midwest, was the leading pork-packing center.

Drovers (drō′vərz) were responsible for bringing the hogs to market. One man wrote: "The ringing crack of the whip and the whoop of the driver in our streets reminds us that the Hog season is again upon us." Before the railroads came, drovers would drive the hogs, sometimes as many as 1,000 at a time, from Indianapolis to Cincinnati.

Sawmills were another familiar sight. This industry came about naturally as a result of the many forests in Indiana. Once the sawmills were in business, settlers no longer had to depend on logrollings to build their cabins and barns. They could buy lumber in sizes they needed from the sawmills. Small factories bought lumber from the sawmills, and began to make furniture and barrels and cut logs for trains and steamers to use for fuel.

The pioneer farmed his land with such simple tools as hoes and sickles and shovels. Everything was done slowly, and with back-breaking toil. Planting, cultivating, harvesting and threshing all had to be done by hand. Farmers had to walk behind their plows to guide them, even though they were pulled by work horses or oxen.

The New Machines

Men with clever minds tried to help the farmer. Soon simple machines were invented to make the work easier. For example, the wooden horse rake, which came out in 1840, made it possible for one man with one horse to do as much work as eight men using hand rakes.

Men were always looking for new ways to make farm work lighter. By 1850, many new machines, all horse-drawn, were on the market. Corn planters, mowers and hay bailers were just a few of the machines that made the farmer's job easier and faster. In time, of course, machines replaced horses. On today's modern farms, one man can plow more ground and plant more seed in a single day than the pioneer farmer, with help, could manage in a whole season.

The Plow

One of the most important tools the farmer uses is the plow. With the plow he breaks the ground, getting it ready for the planting of his crops. At the same time, the plow destroys weeds and circulates air in the soil.

Even in ancient times, farmers used plows. They were just simple wooden tools and did not turn the ground too well. But they were better than no plows at all.

For the early settler, plowing the ground was perhaps his hardest task. One man had this to say about "breaking the land," as he called it. "That first year's plowing," he said, "was enough to ruin the disposition of a preacher. With roots a popping and a cracking and flying back on your shins, dragging the heavy old plow around those green stumps, the clearing was a hairy, scratched-over mess when you were done. It looked more like a bunch of hogs had been rooting there."

Plowing a field filled with roots, rocks and stumps

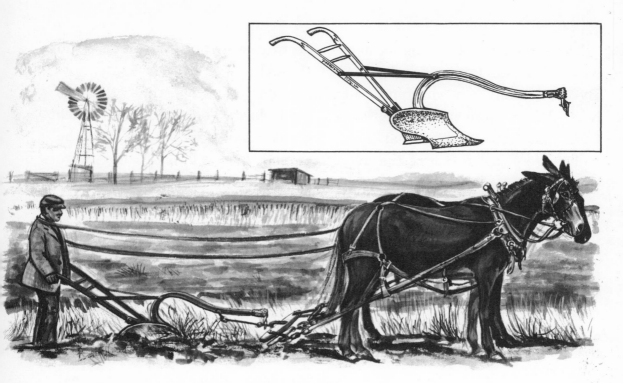

James Oliver's chilled plow

James Oliver

But though the farmers didn't know it yet, better plows were on their way. A man named James Oliver would one day give the farmer a good plow.

James Oliver, who was born in Scotland, did not arrive in Indiana until 1837, when he was thirteen. His father brought the family to a village called Mishawaka (mish'ə-wô′kə). There, James went to school for one year, but left when his father died. Before long, young James found a job in a small iron mill. He became very interested in this work.

When he was grown, James Oliver became part owner of another small iron mill, in what was then the new town of South Bend. He paid less than $90 for his share of the mill, which made cast-iron plows.

Before cast-iron plows were made, farmers had used a bar-shave plow and, later, the shovel plow. The bar-shave plow was a big, awkward tool to handle.

Pioneer farmers used to make jokes about it, saying: "A bar-shave would kick a man over the fence and kick him after he was over!"

The cast-iron plows were better, but they were very heavy. Dirt stuck to the plows slowing them as they moved through the soil.

154

The Chilled Plow

For twelve years after James Oliver became part owner of the mill, he experimented, trying to produce a superior plow. At last he was successful. Dirt did not stick so easily to the Oliver plow, which was known as the chilled plow. It cut smooth, even furrows and could be used in any kind of soil. Best of all, it did not cost very much.

Farmers everywhere wanted the chilled plow. Soon the Oliver Chilled Plow Works, as the mill was soon called, began to supply plows to farmers all over the Midwest. Word of the new plow spread. After a while James Oliver sold thousands of his chilled plows to farmers in Europe, too.

Other Farm Inventions

The inventions came one after another. In early days, planting seed was an endless job. Moving a step at a time, the farmer would drop seed into the ground and then hoe soil over it. Soon machines made it possible for the farmer to measure off a space, drop seed, turn the soil over and even fertilize it, all at the same time. In modern times, airplanes have been used to drop seed over a large area.

Long ago, all farmers picked their corn by hand. Neighbors joined in cornhusking bees to make a happy get-together out of a hard chore. Then machines were invented that not only picked the ears of corn from the stalks, but husked and shelled them, too.

Changes in the Home

While changes were taking place out in the fields, things were also happening in the home. Machine sewing took the place of hand sewing. Butter could be churned by machine. There were even washing machines for those who could afford them. But the invention the women welcomed most of all was the stove.

Stoves were not a new idea. In some countries in Europe, like Germany and Holland, stoves were in use by the end of the Middle Ages.

In America, Benjamin Franklin had invented a stove as early as 1740. But pioneer women still used fireplaces for cooking and heating. When the box cooking stove came along, the women gladly gave up cooking at the fireplace.

The box stove was made of iron. It had a large oven below, and on top there were round pot holes. Wood was burned in the stove,

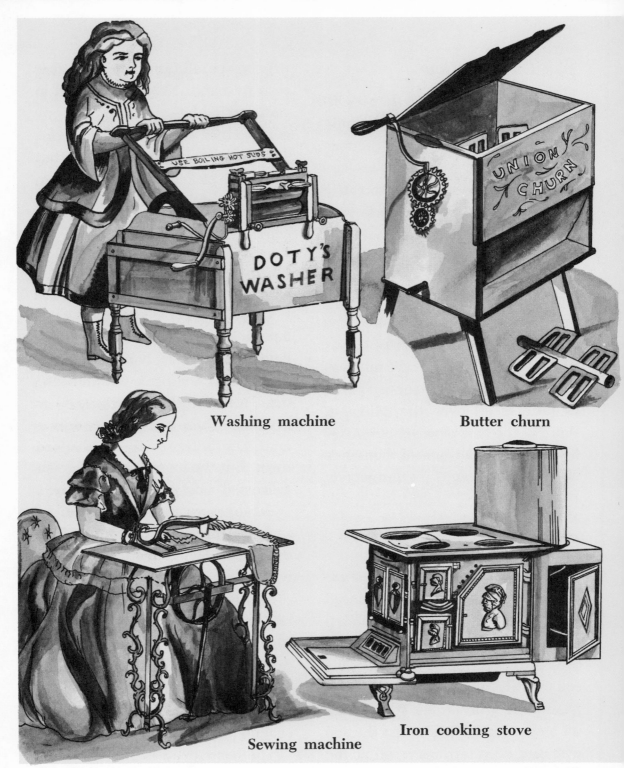

USE BOILING HOT SUDS

DOTY'S WASHER

UNION CHURN

Washing machine

Butter churn

Sewing machine

Iron cooking stove

though later on, coal was used as well. Today, with our modern electric and gas appliances, the old-fashioned stove seems strange and quite funny. But it was a thing of wonder to the women of those days.

The "Iron Horse"

All of these were inventions for the home and the farm. But the minds of men were busy in many other ways, too. One of the areas that concerned inventors was transportation. Traveling by boat or buggy was too slow. Then a new means of transportation appeared that was to change the traveling and transporting habits of America.

People laughed when they first saw the "iron horse." Many people were suspicious of trains. When they learned that trains could travel as fast as twenty miles an hour, they said that the human body was not made to travel at such a terrible speed!

The first railroad in Indiana was started in 1835 in Madison. Twelve years later, it was finished in Indianapolis.

Trains were very different from the ones we know today. They were often given names, like "Ten-Minute-a-Mile Scooter," or "Screech Owl," or "Wild Cat." Schedules were printed, but not followed. Trains made many stops and not always for a good reason. For example, people who lived along the way often flagged down trains so they could talk a while! One woman stopped a train to ask the conductor if he could change a five-dollar bill for her. Passengers complained that the train stopped too often for water. Water for the locomotive was often scooped up in buckets from streams nearby. The engineers called this "jerking water." In later years, when railroads became better, small stations were known as "jerkwater" stops.

Early passenger trains were made in Madison and were thought to be very "elegant." In 1852, a Madison newspaper wrote about the trains. It said: "Mirrors at each end of the cars are provided for the double purpose of ornament and to show how ugly lady or gentlemen passengers are when they behave rudely. We know of no better plan than to put a rude ill-behaved passenger in front of a looking-glass, so that he 'sees himself as others see him.'"

When the first train arrived in Indianapolis, on October 1, 1847, there was a big celebration. A band played, volunteer firemen paraded and a circus entertained the crowds that came to see this new wonder.

Railroads were not invented in the United States. They first appeared in England and were in use there in 1825. In the United States, the first successful railroad was not used until 1832.

Some early automobiles manufactured in Indiana

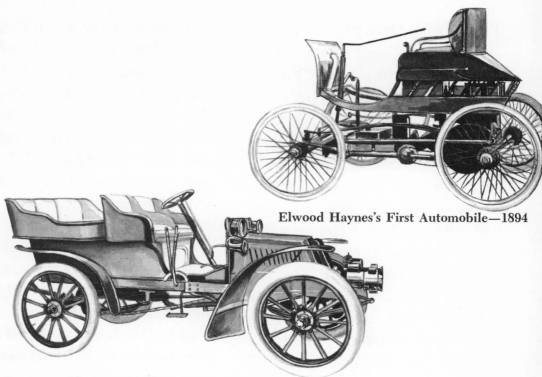

Elwood Haynes's First Automobile—1894

The First Apperson Automobile—1902

Duesenberg Roadster—1921

National Electric Runabout—1903

Railroads made a tremendous difference in the lives of the people. Now Indiana farmers could ship their produce to the east. And they could buy merchandise from other states. As the railroads grew in number, business and industry grew, too.

The Horseless Carriage

Along with railroads, another invention soon changed the face of the nation. This was the automobile.

One of the first automobiles in the United States was made by Elwood Haynes, who lived in Kokomo, Indiana. He designed what he called a "horseless carriage." He went to two mechanics, the Apperson brothers, and paid them forty cents an hour to work on his new machine.

On July 4, 1894, Elwood Haynes tried out his horseless carriage on Pumpkinvine Pike, near Kokomo. And it worked! Four years later, Elwood Haynes formed a company,

with the Apperson brothers, to manufacture automobiles. Elwood Haynes was not the only man to become interested in this new means of transportation. In South Bend, at that time, the Studebaker brothers ran a blacksmith shop. Henry and Clem Studebaker, like other blacksmiths, could make many things. It wasn't long before they were asked to make wagons. Soon the Studebaker brothers gave up the blacksmith shop and went into the wagon business.

They made many wagons for the United States, especially during the Civil War. They became very successful. In 1900, the Studebaker Company was the largest wagon company in the world.

By this time, the Studebaker brothers had become very much interested in the new horseless carriage. Soon they began to manufacture automobiles. But to be on the safe side, they continued to make wagons in addition to automobiles.

The Apperson auto works in 1914

The Interurban (ĭn′tər-ûr′bən)

Within the cities, there was transportation of a different kind. To go from one part of the city to another, people traveled on horse-drawn or mule-drawn streetcars.

These streetcars were in use in Indianapolis during the Civil War. Later other cities in Indiana had horse-drawn streetcars, too.

By 1900, the horse-drawn car had given way to the electrified trolley car. The interurban, which is another word for "between cities," followed the electric trolley. On the interurban, people could travel from one city to another.

The first interurban line connected Anderson and Alexandria. Others soon followed. In the next thirty years, more than 175 towns and cities were connected by the interurban lines. For the first time, Indiana had a transportation system within the state that was fast and reliable.

As trucks and buses came into use, however, the interurban faded away. And when it became common for many families to own their own cars, the interurban lines passed completely out of use. Buses, trucks and automobiles brought a new system of highways in Indiana.

Natural Gas Is Discovered

It was a time of great change, not only in transportation and farming, but in many other ways as well.

Gas had been found in large quantities in Ohio. It was believed that this great natural resource might be found in Indiana, also. Soon wells were being bored into the ground. And gas was discovered!

Some people were not certain about this new fuel. They said the new fuel was the "work of the devil" and refused to have anything to do with it. But others were excited. They came from miles around to see the gas flaming in the air. It was a terrible waste of fuel, but at that time, it was supposed the supply of gas would go on forever.

New businesses sprang up wherever there was a gas supply. One of these was the glass industry. The Ball brothers, who became world-famous for their mason jars, built a factory in Muncie in 1888.

By 1900, unfortunately, the natural supply of gas almost disappeared. Factories that had been using gas were forced to change over to coal.

Most of the factories were in southern Indiana. But soon manufacturers were moving to northern

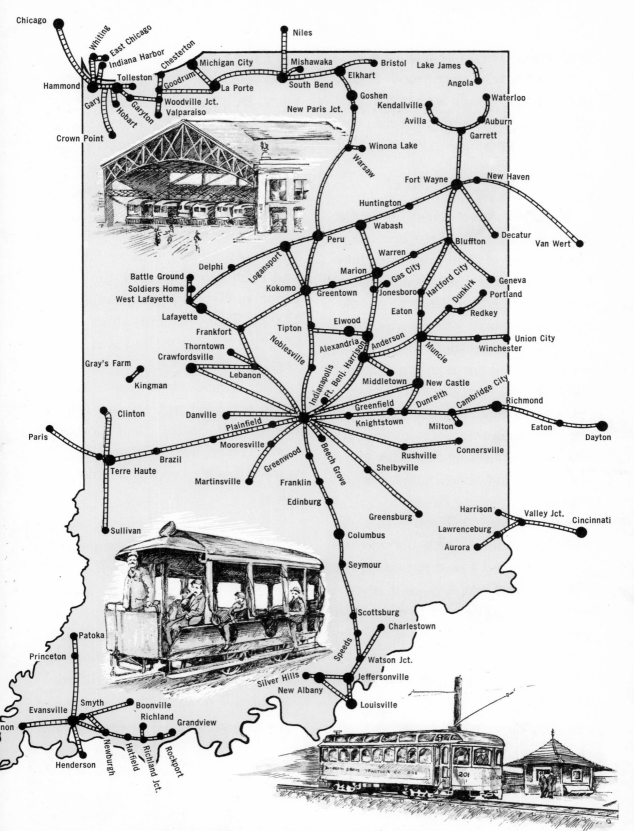

Chicago
Whiting
East Chicago
Indiana Harbor
Chesterton
Michigan City
Niles
Mishawaka
Bristol
Lake James
Angola
Hammond
Tolleston
Goodrum
La Porte
South Bend
Elkhart
Waterloo
Gary
Garyton
Woodville Jct.
Goshen
Kendallville
Avilla
Auburn
Hobart
Valparaiso
New Paris Jct.
Garrett
Crown Point
Winona Lake
Warsaw
Fort Wayne
New Haven
Huntington
Wabash
Decatur
Peru
Van Wert
Delphi
Logansport
Warren
Bluffton
Geneva
Battle Ground
Marion
Gas City
Hartford City
Portland
Soldiers Home
Kokomo
Greentown
Jonesboro
Dunkirk
West Lafayette
Eaton
Redkey
Lafayette
Tipton
Elwood
Frankfort
Noblesville
Alexandria
Harrison
Anderson
Muncie
Union City
Thorntown
Winchester
Gray's Farm
Crawfordsville
Lebanon
Indianapolis
Ft. Benj. Harrison
Middletown
New Castle
Cambridge City
Kingman
Danville
Greenfield
Dunreith
Richmond
Clinton
Plainfield
Knightstown
Milton
Paris
Mooresville
Eaton
Brazil
Greenwood
Rushville
Connersville
Dayton
Terre Haute
Beech Grove
Shelbyville
Martinsville
Franklin
Edinburg
Harrison
Valley Jct.
Greensburg
Lawrenceburg
Cincinnati
Sullivan
Columbus
Aurora
Seymour
Scottsburg
Charlestown
Speeds
Patoka
Watson Jct.
Princeton
Silver Hills
Jeffersonville
New Albany
Evansville
Smyth
Boonville
Louisville
Richland
Grandview
non
Henderson
Newburgh
Hatfield
Richland Jct.
Rockport

Indiana's interurban lines, 1893-1941.

161

Indiana as well. For iron and steel had begun to replace wood. Manufacturers still made farm machinery. But now they were making other products for people in cities as well.

The New Age of Steel

Perhaps the most dramatic change that took place because of the new age of steel was in northern Indiana. Until 1890, the shore of Lake Michigan was almost deserted. Only a few small villages were to be found along the shore line.

This area, known as the Calumet Region, was very close to Chicago. Few people lived there, and land was cheap. New steel mills just going into business decided this was a good place for their huge mills and furnaces.

One of the steel companies decided to build a town outside the mill. It formed a new company, the Gary Land Company, and invited workers to come and live on their land. The first man to come was Thomas Knotts, who brought his family in a wagon and pitched a tent for them to live in.

Thomas Knotts arrived in May, 1906. He was the first settler in Gary. But one short month later, a small village had sprung up. In June, 1906, more than 300 people were living in Gary. Three years later, Gary was a booming frontier town.

Roads were built to connect Gary with other cities, such as Chicago and Hammond. By 1910, the population of Gary had reached almost 17,000. This was only four years after the first settler had pitched his tent!

The largest steel plant in the world was built in Gary in 1906, by the United States Steel Corporation. Today, Gary is one of the world's leading capitals in steel and oil.

Indiana today is an important manufacturing state. And it is still one of the leading farming states in America, too.

Because of invention and industry, Indiana grew from a farming state to become the industrial "crossroads of the nation."

Steel making

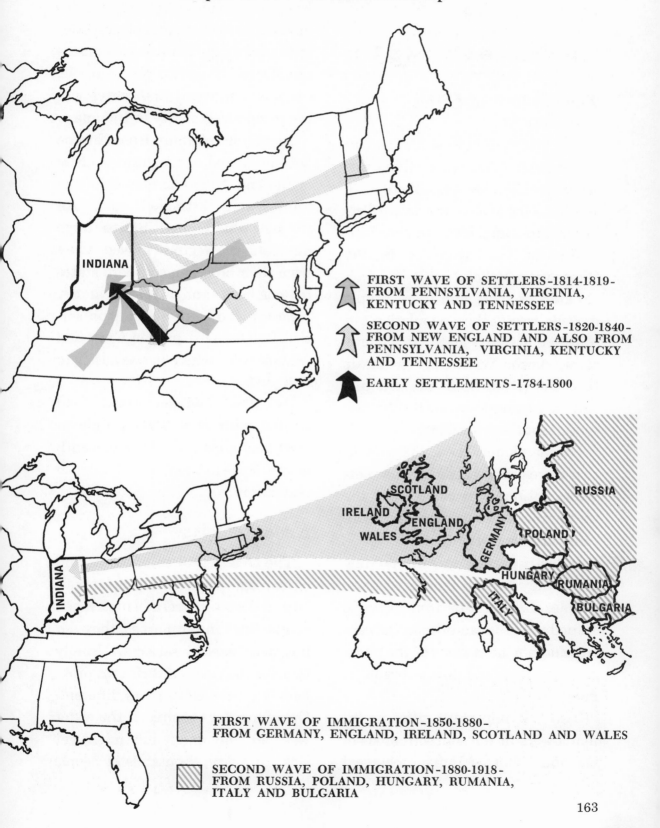

FIRST WAVE OF SETTLERS–1814-1819–
FROM PENNSYLVANIA, VIRGINIA,
KENTUCKY AND TENNESSEE

SECOND WAVE OF SETTLERS–1820-1840–
FROM NEW ENGLAND AND ALSO FROM
PENNSYLVANIA, VIRGINIA, KENTUCKY
AND TENNESSEE

EARLY SETTLEMENTS–1784-1800

FIRST WAVE OF IMMIGRATION–1850-1880–
FROM GERMANY, ENGLAND, IRELAND, SCOTLAND AND WALES

SECOND WAVE OF IMMIGRATION–1880-1918–
FROM RUSSIA, POLAND, HUNGARY, RUMANIA,
ITALY AND BULGARIA

19

Our State Grows Up

The Growth of Cities and Towns

The first American settlement in Indiana was Clarksville, which was settled in 1784. By 1800, there were about 2,500 people in the entire Territory. Most families lived near Vincennes or Clarksville or in the Whitewater Valley.

Later, as more and more people moved west, the population in southern Indiana grew. Most newcomers to the Territory settled near the Ohio River. So at first the history of Indiana was mostly the history of southern Indiana.

During pioneer days, the population increased even more. New settlers continued to come from the southern states, but more and more came also from the east.

Industries grew larger. As they grew, they needed more and more people. Immigrants from Europe settled near the factories in the central and northern parts of the state. And so cities and towns began to grow, too.

The first important cities in Indiana were in the southern areas of the state. But as Indiana changed from an agricultural state to an industrial state, more and bigger cities appeared in the central and northern areas. By 1960, for example, Gary, an important steel center, was the second largest city in Indiana.

Just as immigrants from Europe were attracted to the growing cities of Indiana, Negro families from the south were attracted, too. All through the United States large numbers of Negroes moved away from their homes in southern states to northern and western states. Negroes who came to Indiana settled for the most part in Gary and Indianapolis, where it was easier to find jobs.

By 1960, Indiana, which had started with only 2,500 people in 1800, had grown to be the eleventh largest state in the United States in population.

New Problems

The steady growth of towns and cities created new problems for both city and state governments. When people lived in farm areas, they did not need special services. Usually families took care of their own problems. But in a city, it was different. On a farm, for example, if the water was bad, only one family might get sick. In a city, thousands of people

Early volunteer firemen had only leather buckets and ladders for fighting fires.

could become ill. A fire on a farm might destroy one or two buildings. In a city, whole blocks might go up in flames. And, where so many people were crowded together, disease could spread as quickly as fire.

These and many other problems had to be solved by the city and state governments. Special services had to be created to guard the health of the people. Sewers were made to carry away waste products, water was purified, a garbage collection system was set up, hospitals were built.

Both the cities and the state had to give their citizens some means of transportation to get to and from their jobs. And it became the responsibility of the local governments

to provide recreational facilities for the people as well.

With the growth of the cities, Indiana was faced too with the problems of slums and poverty and crime. Now a police force was needed to protect the citizens from those people who broke the law. A fire department was needed to control and fight fires.

At first fire companies were made up of volunteers. The volunteers were citizens who came running to help when they heard the fire alarm. Then in 1826, in Indianapolis, the first fire company was organized. They had leather buckets and ladders as their only equipment. The fire alarm was given by having

INDIANA'S AIRPORTS AND RAILROADS

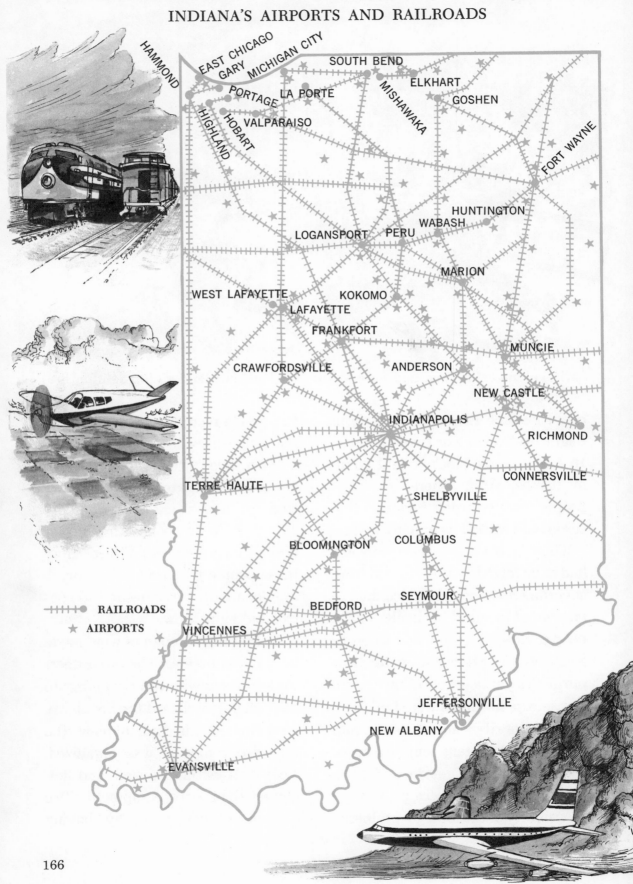

HAMMOND

EAST CHICAGO
GARY
MICHIGAN CITY
SOUTH BEND
ELKHART
GOSHEN
PORTAGE
LA PORTE
MISHAWAKA
HIGHLAND
HOBART
VALPARAISO

FORT WAYNE

HUNTINGTON
WABASH
LOGANSPORT
PERU

MARION

WEST LAFAYETTE
KOKOMO
LAFAYETTE
FRANKFORT

MUNCIE

CRAWFORDSVILLE
ANDERSON

NEW CASTLE

INDIANAPOLIS
RICHMOND

CONNERSVILLE

TERRE HAUTE
SHELBYVILLE

COLUMBUS
BLOOMINGTON

SEYMOUR
BEDFORD
VINCENNES

JEFFERSONVILLE
NEW ALBANY

EVANSVILLE

++|||+ ● **RAILROADS**
★ **AIRPORTS**

someone run and ring a church bell loud and long.

Cities and towns had to be zoned, too. This meant that planning experts had to decide which parts of a city could be used for business, for homes, for schools and so on.

As time went by, towns and cities became overcrowded. In Indiana, as in the rest of the United States, many people found they were not satisfied with city life. They wanted to go on working in the cities, but they no longer wanted to live in them. So they began to move to areas outside the cities, close enough so they could get to work easily, but far enough to feel they were away from city life.

The new areas were called suburbs (sŭb'ûrbz). The word "sub" means "next to" or "outside of." The word "urba" means "city." A suburb, therefore, is a place next to or outside of a city.

But the increase in population and the growth of industry were not the only reasons our state grew.

The Change in Transportation

New and better ways of transportation, faster systems of communication, modern inventions helped Indiana grow, too.

Roads changed from Indian trails and dirt paths into smooth, paved superhighways. These superhighways joined Indiana to her sister states. Today cars, trucks and buses move swiftly where once wagon trains crossed the land.

In 1850, there were only a few miles of railroad in Indiana. The railroad between Indianapolis and Madison had just been finished. Trains were slow. In those days, a man on a horse could race a train and win! Now a network of railroads connects Indiana with the rest of the nation in speedy and safe transportation of freight and passengers.

Today, too, jet planes fly in and out of modern airports in Indiana, at a speed that would have amazed the men who flew the first airplane on a cold winter day in 1903.

The Change in Communication

As transportation improved, communication improved rapidly, too. In early days, letters were delivered by horseback and stage coach. When railroads came into use, mail was sent in mail cars. Then the telegraph was invented. Messages could be sent and received instantly with the telegraph. Soon there was a telegraph network covering Indiana.

The telephone was invented in 1879. Only a few years later, the telephone was being used in all the cities and, shortly afterward, in farm areas as well. Everyone thought the telephone was the best invention of all, for now people could talk directly to each other over long distances.

Another wonderful invention that changed the lives of people was the radio. At first only signals in code were sent out. But soon the human voice itself was heard. When this happened, it was not long before news from around the world was reported almost the moment it was taking place. Farmers in the most distant and lonely parts of Indiana knew what was happening in the world as soon as the city people did.

With the invention of television, people were drawn even closer together. Today, one can see and hear people in other parts of the world, live, at the moment they are speaking, through the use of communication satellites (săt'ə-līts), such as Telestar. And television plays an important part in education.

Indiana's State Parks

During the 1920's, Indiana, along with the rest of the nation, was prosperous. This meant that times were good, people had money to spend and jobs were easy to find. During this time, Indiana started a state park system that made Indiana a leader among the other states. A man named Richard Lieber was responsible for the new and better state park system.

Today there are almost 30 state parks and forests throughout Indiana which offer all kinds of activities, such as swimming, fishing, hiking and boating. Some state parks are historic sites, such as the Lincoln Pioneer Village, the pioneer village in Spring Mill park, and the mounds at Anderson State Park.

The Great Depression

In the 1930's Indiana as well as the rest of the U.S., was hurt by the depression. The depression, which began in 1929, was a time when men could not get jobs. Farmers could not sell their products. Many businesses failed, which threw even more people out of work. People did not have money to buy anything. Many families could not even buy enough food. The United States government passed many laws, trying to help the nation recover from the depression.

When the depression was over, Indiana made great progress as a

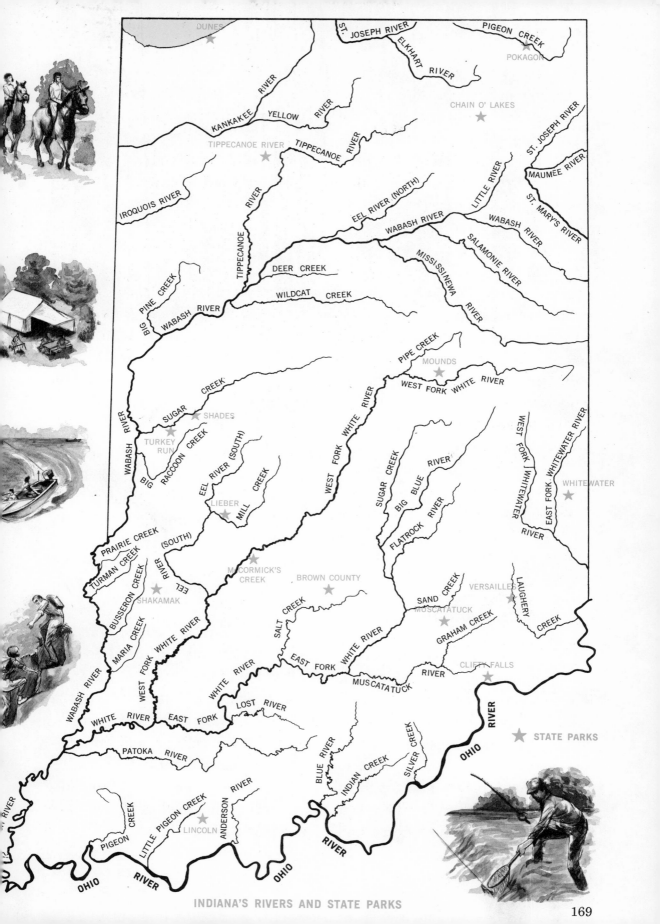

INDIANA'S RIVERS AND STATE PARKS

169

Clowes Hall, home of the Indianapolis Symphony Orchestra and
the Metropolitan Opera National Company

manufacturing state. The city of Indianapolis became an important center for industry and trade. Today, Indiana is one of the eight most important states in industry, as well as farming.

Progress in Indiana

As Indiana made progress in industry, in farming and in education, it progressed in culture, too. Indianapolis has a fine symphony orchestra, which gives special concerts for children as a regular feature.

Fine museums are also found in Indiana. In Indianapolis, there is a special Children's Museum, as well as the John Herron Art Institute. Fort Wayne has an Art School and Museum. There is a museum in Evansville and an art gallery in Terre Haute. And many artists work and live in the beautiful wooded hills and valleys of Brown County.

Indiana has 247 public libraries. Both the Indiana Historical Society Library and the library of the Indiana Academy of Science are in the State Library at Indianapolis. Many of our colleges and universities have large libraries.

Our state has grown up, but Indiana will go on growing. Indiana has a bright future.

Places of Interest in Indiana

1. **Battle Ground**
   scene of the Battle of Tippecanoe
2. **Bloomington**
   Indiana Museum of Art
   Indiana University
   Indiana University Museum
3. **Brookville**
   Whitewater Canal
4. **Corydon**
   2nd territorial capitol and
   1st state capitol
5. **Crawfordsville**
   home of Henry S. Lane
   home of Lew Wallace
6. **Evansville**
   Mesker Zoo
   Museum of Arts and Sciences
7. **Fort Wayne**
   Fort Wayne Art Museum
   grave of Johnny Appleseed
8. **Fountain City**
   home of Levi Coffin
9. **Greenfield**
   home of James Whitcomb Riley
10. **Hanover**
    Hanover College, Geology Museum
11. **Indianapolis**
    Children's Museum
    Clowes Hall, home of the Indianap-
      olis Symphony Orchestra and the
      Metropolitan Opera National Com-
      pany
    Herron Museum of Art
    home of President
      Benjamin Harrison
    Indiana Historical Society Library
    Indiana Soldiers' and Sailors'
      Monument
    Indiana State Capitol
    Indiana State Museum
    Indianapolis Motor Speedway,
      home of the 500-mile race
    Lockerbie home of
      James Whitcomb Riley
    World War Memorial Plaza
12. **Lafayette**
    Lafayette Art Center
    Purdue University
13. **Lincoln City**
    Nancy Hanks Lincoln
    State Memorial
14. **Madison**
    home of James Lanier
15. **Mishawaka**
    Mishawaka Children's Museum
16. **Mitchell**
    restored pioneer village
17. **Muncie**
    Ball State Teachers' Art Gallery
    Ball State University
18. **Newburgh**
    Angel Mounds
19. **New Harmony**
    New Harmony National
      Historic Landmark
20. **Richmond**
    Art Association of Richmond
      (art gallery)

Joseph Moore Museum
      of Earlham College
21. **Rockport**
    Lincoln pioneer village
22. **Santa Claus**
    home of Toy Village
23. **South Bend**
    University of Notre Dame
      Art Gallery
    South Bend Art Center
24. **Terre Haute**
    Indiana State University
    Sheldon Swope Art Gallery
25. **Vincennes**
    1st territorial capitol building
    George Rogers Clark Memorial
    home of William Henry Harrison
26. **Wyandotte**
    Wyandotte Cave

171

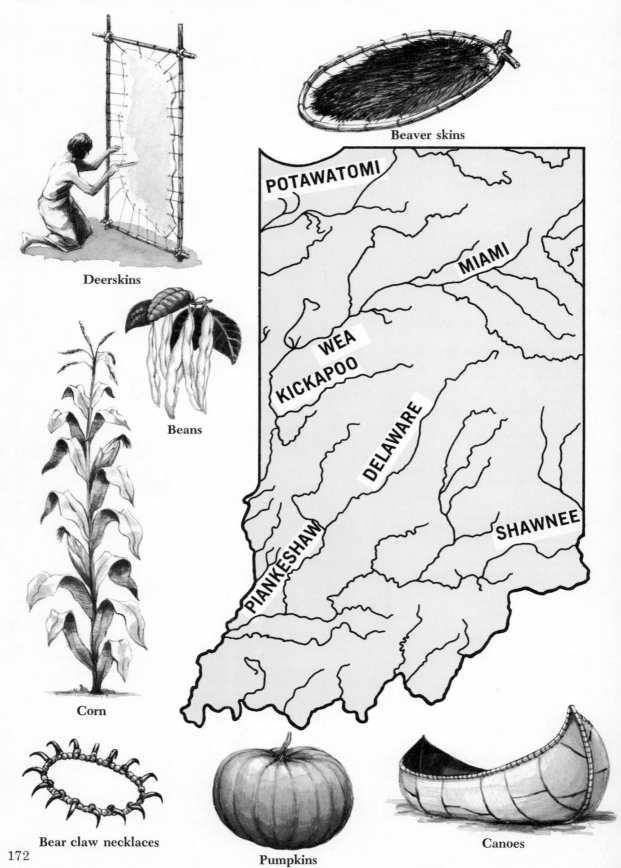

Deerskins

Beaver skins

Beans

Corn

Bear claw necklaces

Pumpkins

Canoes

POTAWATOMI

MIAMI

WEA

KICKAPOO

DELAWARE

PIANKESHAW

SHAWNEE

172

Indiana's Indian Tribes, 1750-1800, and some products of their civilization.

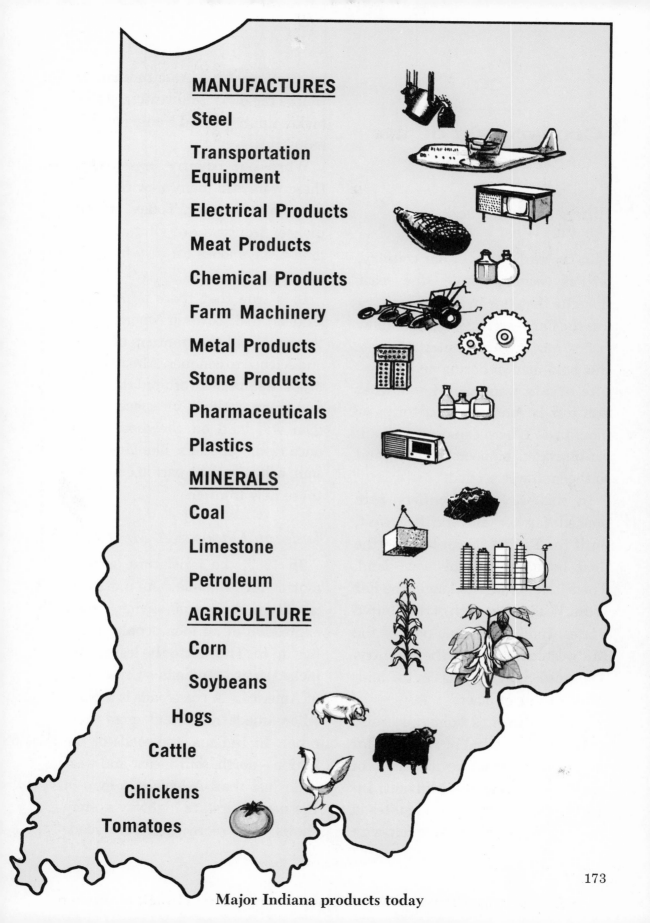

MANUFACTURES

Steel

Transportation Equipment

Electrical Products

Meat Products

Chemical Products

Farm Machinery

Metal Products

Stone Products

Pharmaceuticals

Plastics

MINERALS

Coal

Limestone

Petroleum

AGRICULTURE

Corn

Soybeans

Hogs

Cattle

Chickens

Tomatoes

173

Major Indiana products today

20

Crossroads of the Nation

When Indiana was the Far West

In the early days of our country, settlers coming from the east thought that the Indiana Territory was the Far West. They did not know at first how large a country this was. But bold men of daring and adventure always wanted to know what was just beyond the next forest or mountain. Where explorers and adventurers led, pioneers followed, and so the land was settled.

In this way the frontiers were pushed farther and farther west, until the Pacific Ocean became the final boundary to this vast land. Then Indiana was no longer the Far West. With the growth of the United States, Indiana became part of the Midwestern area of the country. The word "mid" means "in the middle of a thing or place."

The Midwest is sometimes also called the heartland of America, for the most important farming areas of the nation are in the Midwest. Indiana, along with her sister states in this region, supplies America with much of its food. And Indiana, as well as the other Midwestern states, makes up the second leading area in industry.

When our country was young, there were still many new frontiers for men to conquer. Today, the old pioneer frontiers are all gone. But man always looks for new frontiers to explore.

It is true that there is no more land left to discover in America. But there are still the frontiers of space and science to conquer. Already men in space ships have orbited the earth and even walked in space. Soon men will land on the moon. And once again Hoosiers, like Gus Grissom, will take their part in exploring these new frontiers.

Indiana Chooses A Motto

In 1937, the legislature chose a motto for Indiana. A motto is usually a short true saying, or an expression of an idea people try to live up to. The motto the legislature picked was "Indiana—Crossroads of America." A crossroads is a place where roads meet and cross each other. In Indiana, the roads of the nation—north, south, east and west—do just that. A look at a map of the new interstate highway system shows that more interstate roads

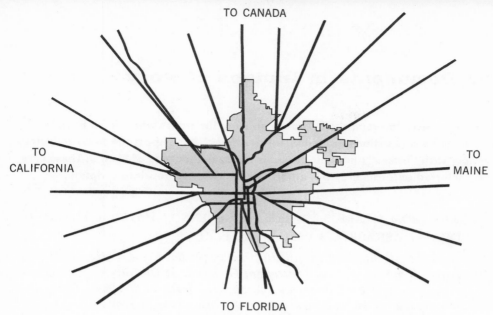

TO CANADA

TO CALIFORNIA

TO MAINE

TO FLORIDA

Indianapolis—Crossroads of the Nation

cross at Indianapolis than in any other city.

Famous Men in Indiana History

From our state—truly the crossroads of America—have come men and inventions to enrich, strengthen and change the land. Explorers like George Rogers Clark, dreamers like Robert Owen, inventors like Elwood Haynes and Wilbur Wright all helped to make our country great.

From the crossroads of America have come writers, musicians and artists. A Hoosier scientist, Herman Mueller, won a Nobel Prize. A Hoosier architect, Alexander Ralston, helped plan the nation's capital in Washington, D.C. Indiana sent a president, Benjamin Harrison, to the White House. And it was in Indiana that Abraham Lincoln, who freed the slaves and saved the Union, spent his important growing and learning years.

This book began with prehistoric times, before there were maps, and before Indiana had its own place on maps of the world. It finishes with an Indiana grown strong, and still growing, in the heart of a strong and proud United States.

But history does not come to an end when this book is closed and put aside. Each day that we live is the history of tomorrow. And the children of today are the men and women of tomorrow who will write their own history as they live it.

History is the record of what man has done. In future records, as in the past, the state of Indiana is sure to write an exciting story.

Historic Documents in Indiana History

A great historian remarked, "Documents are the traces which have been left by the thoughts and actions of men of former time." It is impossible to write history without such "traces" and their use adds flavor to the study of history. These carefully selected excerpts may be integrated with the appropriate chapters.

EXCERPT FROM CLARK'S LETTER TO GOVERNOR PATRICK HENRY OF VIRGINIA—KASKASKIA, FEBRUARY 3, 1779

Clark had recently learned through a friendly trader, Francis Vigo, that General Henry Hamilton, British Lieutenant Governor at Detroit, had recaptured Vincennes and held Fort Sackville there with a force of 600 men. Convinced that his only chance lay in a surprise march through the flooded and icy wilderness against Fort Sackville, Clark prepared a little army of approximately 170 men. 130 men, led by Clark, went overland; 40 were sent by river. The following is taken from the report sent to Governor Henry before his departure for Vincennes. This campaign stands as one of the most daring exploits in American history.

. . . without a reinforcement . . . I shall be obliged to give up this country to Mr. Hamilton. . . . I am resolved to take the advantage of his present situation and risk the whole on a single battle. I shall set out in a few days with all the force I can raise of my own troops and a few militia that I can depend on. . . .

. . . I know the case is desperate, but Sr, we must either quit the country or attack Mr. Hamilton. No time is to be lost. Was I sure of a reinforcement, I should not attempt it. Who knows what fortune will do for us? Great things have been effected by a few men well conducted. Perhaps we may be fortunate. We have this consolation; that our cause is just and that our country will be grateful and not con[demn] our conduct in case we fail, though, if so, this coun[try] as well as Kentucky, I believe, is lost.

THE NORTHWEST ORDINANCE, 1787

A committee had submitted a report to Congress on the government of the western territory on April 23, 1784. It was largely based on a plan proposed by Thomas Jefferson although the anti-slavery provision he advocated was defeated by a vote of seven states to six. The interest of the Ohio Company in colonizing the Ohio Country led Congress to enact a definitive plan of government on July 13, 1787. In the initial stage the Northwest Ordinance provided for a highly centralized government with no popular participation. A legislature, elected with property qualifications, was authorized when the Territory's male population numbered five thousand adults. The governor was given an absolute veto. But the ordinance included a prohibition against slavery, provision for a democratic system of inheritance, and a bill of rights. No less than three nor more than five states should be formed from the territory. A minimum population of sixty thousand was required for statehood.

It is hereby Ordained and declared by the authority aforesaid, That the following Articles shall be considered as Articles of compact between the Original States and the people and States in the said territory, and forever remain unalterable, unless by common consent, *to wit*,

Article the First. No person demeaning himself in a peaceable and orderly manner shall ever be molested on account of his mode of worship or religious sentiments in the said territory.

Article the Second. The Inhabitants of the said territory shall always be entitled to the benefits of the writ of habeas corpus, and of the trial by Jury; of a proportionate representation of the people in the legislature, and of judicial proceedings according to the course of the common law; all persons shall be bailable unless for capital offenses, where the proof shall be evident, or the presumption great; all fines shall be moderate, and no cruel or unusual punishments shall be inflicted; no man shall be deprived of his liberty or property but by the judgment of his peers, or the law of the land; and should the public exigencies make it necessary for the common preservation to take any persons property, or to demand his particular services, full compensation shall be made for the same; and in the just preservation of rights and property it is understood and declared; that no law ought ever to be made, or have force in the said territory, that shall in any manner whatever interfere with, or affect private contracts or engagements, bona fide and without fraud previously formed.

Article the Third. Religion, Morality and knowledge being necessary to good government and the happiness of mankind, Schools and the means of education shall forever be encouraged. The utmost good faith shall always be observed towards the Indians, their lands and property shall never be taken from them without their consent; and in their property, rights and liberty, they never shall be invaded or disturbed, unless in just and lawful wars authorised by Congress; but laws founded in justice and humanity shall from time to time be made, for preventing wrongs being done to them, and for preserving peace and friendship with them.

Article the Fourth. The said territory, and the States which may be formed therein shall forever remain a part of this Confederacy of the United States of America . . . . and whenever any of the said States shall have sixty thousand free Inhabitants therein, such State shall be admitted by its Delegates into the Congress of the United States, on an equal footing with the original States, in all respects whatever; and shall be at liberty to form a permanent constitution and State government, provided the constitution and government so to be formed, shall be republican, and in conformity to the principles contained in these Articles; and so far as it can be consistent with the general interest of the Confederacy, such admission shall be allowed at an earlier period, and when there may be a less number of free Inhabitants in the State than sixty thousand.

Article the Sixth. There shall be neither Slavery nor involuntary Servitude in the said territory otherwise than in the punishment of crimes, whereof the party shall have been duly convicted; provided always that any person escaping into the same, from whom labor or service is lawfully claimed in any one of the original States, such fugitive may be lawfully reclaimed and conveyed to the person claiming his or her labor or service as aforesaid.

Be it Ordained by the Authority aforesaid, that the Resolutions of the 23d of April 1784 relative to the subject of this ordinance be, and the same are hereby repealed and declared null and void. Done &c.

INDIANA'S FIRST CONSTITUTION, 1816

On June 10, 1816, the constitutional delegates assembled at Corydon. As a group they were men of high quality. Of the forty-three elected twenty-six had southern antecedents but had come from the democratic backcountry rather than the plantation tidewater. Eleven were from northern states and six were foreign born. Jonathan Jennings was chosen as president and William Hendricks as secretary of the convention. By a vote of 33 to 8 they asserted that it was expedient to form a constitution. In preparing Indiana's fundamental law they borrowed heavily from existing state constitutions especially those of Virginia, Ohio, and Kentucky. They produced a strongly democratic document for that period which served Indiana well for thirty-five years. Slavery was forbidden and an advanced concept of state responsibility for public education was incorporated. The amending process was to prove cumbersome. The new constitution went into effect without submission to the people.

PREAMBLE

We the Representatives of the people of the Territory of Indiana, in Convention met, at Corydon, on monday the tenth day of June in the year of our Lord eighteen hundred and sixteen, and of the Independence of the United States, the fortieth, having the right of admission into the General Government, as a member of the union, consistent with the constitution of the United States, the ordinance of Congress of one thousand seven hundred and eighty seven, and the law of Congress, entitled "An act to enable the people of the Indiana Territory to form a Constitution and State Government, and for the admission of such state into the union, on an equal footing with the original States" in order to establish Justice, promote the welfare, and secure the blessings of liberty to ourselves and our posterity; do ordain and establish the following constitution or form of Government, and do mutually agree with each other to form ourselves into a free and Independent state, by the name of the State of Indiana.

ARTICLE I.

Sect. 1st. That the general, great and essential principles of liberty and free Government may be recognized and unalterably established; WE declare, That all men are born equally free and independent, and have certain natural, inherent, and unalienable rights; among which are the enjoying and defending life and liberty, and of acquiring, possessing, and protecting property, and pursuing and obtaining happiness and safety.

Sect. 2. That all power is inherent in the people; and all free Governments are founded on their authority, and instituted for their peace, safety and happiness. For the advancement of these ends, they have at all times an unalienable and indefeasible right to alter or reform their Government in such manner as they may think proper.

Sect. 3. That all men have a natural and indefeasible right to worship Almighty God, according to the dictates of their own consciences: That no man shall be compelled to attend, erect, or support any place of Worship, or to maintain any ministry against his consent: That no human authority can, in any case whatever, control or interfere with the rights of conscience: And that no preference shall ever be given by law to any religious societies, or modes of worship; and no religious test shall be required as a qualification to any office of trust or profit.

Sect. 4. That elections shall be free and equal.

Caleb Mills, the father of common schools, came to Indiana from his native New Hampshire in 1833 to teach at the newly opened Wabash College. He was a passionate advocate for a free public school system and the creation of greater educational opportunities in his adopted state. In 1846, he issued a series of six "messages," which so influenced the state legislature that it finally passed a school law incorporating many of the ideas for which he so vigorously pleaded. The law also provided for community libraries, based on Caleb Mills' contention that libraries were of significant importance in education. The State Teachers Association was founded with Caleb Mills' assistance in 1854. He also served as State Superintendent of Public Instruction for three years, from 1854 to 1857.

Caleb Mills. Sixth Annual Address on Popular Education To the Legislature of Indiana. By one of the people. Five Thousand Copies Printed by Order of the Senate of Indiana. Indianapolis. J. P. Chapman, State Printer. 1852 Address. The Educational Outlook.

The first element of our system of common schools should be *freedom*. They should be accessible to all the youth of our State of suitable age without the intervention of the odious rate bill, or any other let or hindrance. The spirit of our republican institutions requires that these nurseries of true, genuine democracy, should be open to all alike, without regard to any of these factitious distinctions, which wealth and sectarian bigotry create. The ameliorating power of well taught and well governed schools, has been seen and felt in various parts of the land. They contribute more than any other one agency, to mould and assimilate the various discordant materials to be incorporated into the body politic and render them homogeneous in character and sympathy. How often have we all seen in those nurseries of knowledge, aristocratic pride humbled, plebeian roughness refined, rustic conceit corrected, haughty insolence rebuked and repressed, gentle modesty emboldened, unobtrusive worth encouraged, and many of the asperities of character give place to lovelier traits, all contributing to swell the aggregate of human happiness, domestic peace and civil freedom. Their worth and influence on the welfare of society can not be expressed in language, nor represented by any numerical formula. Competent to such results, susceptible of such elevation and subservient to such interests, they ought to be taxed to their utmost capacity, and rendered *free* as the air we breathe, or the sunlight that greets unasked, alike the cottage of the poor and the mansion of the rich.

John V. Beamer served his community, Wabash, and the state in many useful ways. He was a business man, civic leader, state legislator and congressman. His pride in the Hoosier State is evident in this eloquent statement written shortly before his death in 1964.

I am a Hoosier. I was born on July 4, 1800, and I grew to full manhood on December 11, 1816. Our family was small then—only nineteen of us, but that family was a proud and determined one, and I was destined to become an important part of that family of states.

I descended from a hardy stock in the hills of Virginia, North Carolina, and Pennsylvania. I came through the Cumberland Gap, down the beautiful Ohio River, and I found a land of fine hardwoods—popular, oak, and walnut. My first home was made with logs from these trees. Wild animal skins provided the covers for our beds and the clothing and caps to keep our bodies warm.

I believed in freedom then, I believed in it when there was a conflict, and I believe in it today. Abraham Lincoln lived with me for fourteen years, his formative years. Morgan and his raiders visited me. I fought at Shiloh, Gettysburg, Vicksburg, at San Juan Hill, at Chateau Thierry, at the Bulge, and in far away Guam and Korea . . . I stand ready to fight again to retain that freedom.

I am education and enlightment. I live at Bloomington, West Lafayette, Crawfordsville, Greencastle, Franklin, Muncie, Terre Haute, Notre Dame, and in every town and city where there is a grade school, high school, or college.

I learned from the Miamis, the Delawares, Shawnees, Kickopoos, and the Potawatomies. The blood of many nations is in my veins, and the dreams of every youth have been realized by me. The English, Germans, French, Italians, Africans, Orientals, and many others sought and found homes and opportunities with me. They helped me grow in understanding and all of us believe in the universal brotherhood of man.

I have built the best roads, railroads, and canals across the breadth and length of my domain. Overhead I have helped to conquer the forces of gravity and fly as do the birds. I have tunnelled and stripped our hills for coal; I have drilled and found oil. I have corn kings and sun and wind-tanned men who follow the furrow in the rich soils that the Creator gave me. I am the crossroads of America.

The automobile is one of my great inventions. My 500 mile race track is a grand me-

morial to the industry. There are steel mills, oil refineries, and nearly every type of manufacture to bring material comfort and wealth to mankind. I am Elwood Haynes, Studebaker, Oliver, and countless numbers of brave industrialists whose accomplishments are boldly recorded in our economic history.

I am Edward Eggleston and "The Hoosier Schoolmaster," Booth Tarkington, Lew Wallace, Meredith Nicholson, Gene Stratton Porter, George Ade, Kim Hubbard and scores of authors whose pens have given me one of the highest spots in the literary arts.

I have contributed much to the great United States of which I proudly am a part. I have given it the services of the Harrisons— William Henry and Benjamin, of a Fairbanks, Beveridge, Lane, Thomas Marshall, and many others who have served with distinction in the legislative, executive, and judicial branches of our government.

I have dreamed dreams and had visions with George Rogers Clark as he helped to open up a new territory, with George Rapp and Robert Owen as they attempted to establish a Utopia at New Harmony. My prayers always have been to an Almighty Creator.

I am as a child at play, full of hope and expectancy; as an athlete well trained for the challenging contest, as a gladiator girded for the arena, and as an old man full of experiences and understanding.

I believe in our God, the Creator of all good and perfect gifts. My greatest desire is to be helpful to others that they may share the God-given bounties that I am privileged to possess. I pray that we never shall forsake freedom for a dole nor our liberty for a false promise.

—John V. Beamer

GLOSSARY

The Glossary will help you to pronounce hard words correctly and to understand the meanings of some of the words used in this book.

The letters and marks in parentheses following many of the more difficult words will show you how to pronounce these words. A heavy mark like this (′) follows the syllable of a word which has the strongest stress; a lighter mark like this (′) follows a syllable which has a lesser stress. One-syllable words contain no stress marks. Only rather long words with several syllables have both kinds of stress marks.

PRONUNCIATION KEY

ă	hat	j	jar, gem	th	thin
ā	name			t͟h	then
â	care	ŏ	top		
ä	far	ō	so		
ĕ	let	ô	short, call	ŭ	cup
ē	he	oi	oil	ū	music, beauty
		o͝o	look	û	burn, earth
ĭ	bit	o͞o	cool		
ī	bite	ou	about, crowd	zh	vision

ə any vowel not in an accented syllable, as the a in about (ə-bout′) or the e in taken (tā′kən).

abolished (ə-bŏl′ĭsht), did away with; brought to an end.

accidentally, not planned; happening by chance.

activities, certain actions or things to do, such as school *activities*, or sport *activities*.

ammunition (ăm′yə-nĭsh′ən), anything that can be thrown or exploded, such as bombs, gun powder, shells and bullets; any weapon that can be used against an enemy.

amphibians (ăm-fĭb′ĭ-ənz), animals able to live both in the water and on the land.

archaeologist (är′kĭ-ŏl′ə-jĭst), one who studies the life and times of prehistoric people by digging up artifacts and ancient cities; a person who studies ancient times.

auction (ôk′shən), a public sale at which things are sold to those people who pay the most money.

banished, forced to leave a place; made to go away.

barely, only just, as we *barely* got to the train on time.

booming, growing quickly in size and in business.

bored, dug a hole with a tool turning in the ground.

boundary, a line that shows where something ends; a line that divides one thing from another.

britches, pants; trousers.

candidate (kăn′də-dāt′), a person who runs, or is asked to run, for an office or a special honor.

century (sĕn'chə-rĭ), one hundred years.

ceremonies (sĕr'ə-mō'nēz), certain acts done in the same way on special days, as in Indian *ceremonies* before a buffalo hunt; speeches and other actions performed to honor a holiday or other important day, such as *ceremonies* on July 4th.

charred (chärd), burned just a little.

circulates (sûr'kyə-lāts'), moves around from one place to another, or from one person to another.

committed (kə-mĭt'əd), did something wrong, such as stealing.

compass (kŭm'pəs), an instrument in which a moving needle points north; an instrument for showing directions.

concerned (kən-sûrnd'), interested; worried.

conquered (kŏng'kərd), won by force, as in a war.

consolidate (kən-sŏl'ə-dāt'), to bring or join things together; to make one large thing of many small things.

constitution (kŏn'stə-tū'shən), a set of laws, usually written, by which a country is governed; laws based on the ideas people or a nation believe in.

constitutional (kŏn'stə-tū'shən-əl), having to do with the constitution.

controlled (kən-trōld'), had power over; commanded.

cooperated (kō-ŏp'ə-rāt'əd), worked with or helped others willingly.

created (krē-ā'təd), made, usually something new.

crouched (kroucht), bent over low, as if ready to jump.

culture (kŭl'chər), the way people live within a certain time; the habits of a country or group of people, such as the *culture* of the ancient Indians.

current, fast-moving running water, as in a stream or river.

customs, habits; the usual way of acting.

debris (də-brē'), anything left over that is broken or useless; rubbish.

delinquent (dĭ-lĭng'kwənt), a person who acts against the laws of his country; a person who performs acts of mischief or harm to other people or places.

democracy (dĭ-mŏk'rə-sĭ), a government which is ruled by the people.

dense, thick; pushed or crowded together.

designs (dĭ-zīnz'), drawings; special patterns made in such things as pottery, beadwork or cloth.

destination (dĕs'tə-nā'shən), a place at the end of a trip; the place to which a person or thing is going.

dictator (dĭk'tā-tər), a person who has complete power over others.

disposition (dĭs'pə-zĭsh'ən), one's natural way of acting toward others, such as a happy *disposition* or an unpleasant *disposition*.

doubt, to be not certain or sure about something; to find it hard to believe.

downcast, sad; unhappy.

dramatic, exciting; stirring.

drill, to do a thing again and again; in the army, to learn to march, practice using a gun and other duties.

drovers (drō'vərz), men who drive animals, such as hogs, sheep or cattle, to market.

elegant (ĕl'ə-gənt), in fine taste; showing a finer feeling.

enforce, to make someone obey; to force.

equality (ĭ-kwŏl'ə-tĭ), the sameness in things, such as number or size or importance.

equip (ĭ-kwĭp'), to supply whatever is needed.

executive (ĭg-zĕk′yə-tĭv), a person who is in charge; a manager; in government, the person who sees that the laws are put into action.

experiment, a test to discover something.

facilities (fə-sĭl′ə-tēz), things that make work or play easier, such as kitchen *facilities* or park *facilities*.

familiar, something well known; something seen often, as a *familiar* street.

farflung, stretching out over a great distance.

features (fē′chərz), things that are special and noticed, as a house has its good *features* and its bad *features*.

flagged, signaled; got attention by waving a flag or other object.

flint, a very hard stone; a piece of hard stone used for striking against steel to produce sparks or fire.

furrowed (fûr′ōd), made long, deep tracks in the ground with a plow.

generous (jĕn′ər-əs), free and unselfish in giving, as a *generous* gift; giving a large amount; not stingy.

geological (jē′ə-lŏj′ə-kəl), having to do with geology, or earth studies.

geologist (jĭ-ŏl′ə-jəst), one who makes a study of the earth, its composition, especially as seen in rocks, its changes and its history.

grieved (grēvd), felt deep sorrow for.

guided, led the way; showed the way.

hacked, chopped with short, cutting blows.

harmony (här′mə-nĭ), agreement; getting along well together in peace and friendship.

harsh, not kind; rough; severe.

haul, to drag or pull, using force, as to *haul* a heavy wagon.

hindered (hĭn′dərd), held back; stopped; not allowed to go on.

horrified (hôr′ə-fīd′), felt great fear or terror; shocked.

ill-behaved, not polite; behaving in a bad way; without manners.

immigrants (ĭm′ə-grənts), people of one country who move to live the rest of their lives in another country.

implements (ĭm′plə-mənts), tools or instruments.

intensely, very strongly; with very great feeling.

invaded, went in as an enemy; entered by force.

judicial (jōō-dĭsh′əl), having to do with courts of law or with judges.

keen (kēn), biting or sharp, as a *keen* wind; intelligent, as a *keen* mind; sharp, as a *keen* sense of hearing; eager, as *keen* for a sport.

legal (lē′gəl), allowed by law; having to do with the law or those practicing the law.

legend (lĕj′ənd), a story handed down from early days that may or may not be true; a story, usually dealing with a real person or place, which cannot be proved.

leveled (lĕv′əld), made even or flat.

locomotive (lō′kə-mō′tĭv), an engine that can move by itself, usually used to pull the cars of a train.

loft (lôft), a room or space over the top story of a house or building, and under the roof; an attic space.

magnificient (măg-nĭf′ə-sənt), grand; splendid; princely.

manned, supplied with men; operated by men, as the pirate ship was *manned* by fierce fighters.

massacre (măs′ə-kər), the senseless, cruel killing of many people or animals.

mechanics (mə-kăn′ĭks), people who are skilled in handling machines or tools.

merchandise (mûr′chən-dīz′), products, or goods, bought and sold; usually, manufactured products.

method (měth′əd), a planned way of doing things; doing things in an orderly way.

migrations (mī-grā′shənz), the movement of people, or animals, in a large group from one place to another.

mischief, damage; trouble; harm.

missionaries (mĭsh′ə-něr′ēz), people who wish to spread their religion in places where their religion is not known or not generally accepted.

navigating (năv′ə-gā′tĭng), keeping a ship or plane on its course; steering a boat on a river or an ocean.

obstacles (ŏb′stə-kəlz), things that stand in the way; things that keep a person from moving ahead, such as obstacles in the road.

operated, worked, or ran a machine.

opposite (ŏp′ə-zĭt), different as can be; going in different directions, as one plane going north and another south.

ordinance (ôrd′nəns), a law or command; a law made by a government, such as a state ordinance.

organization (ôr′gən-ə-zā′shən), a group of people sharing the same idea or purpose who get together to form a club, such as the boy scouts, or a group of businessmen.

original (ə-rĭj′ə-nəl), the first, as in the original thirteen states; having to do with the beginning of a thing.

ornamental, anything used as an ornament or for decoration.

ornaments, anything used to make things or people look more attractive or beautiful.

parochial (pə-rō′kĭ-əl), having to do with a church area; supported by or having to do with a church.

particular, special; unusual; set apart from others.

patriot (pā′trĭ-ət), a person who loves and stands by his country at all times.

pelts, the skins of small animals, usually animals with fur.

per, for each.

permanent (pûr′mə-nənt), lasting, or meant to last for a long, long time; unchanging; always the same.

pictorial (pĭk-tōr′ĭ-əl), having to do with pictures, such as a pictorial history book.

plundered (plŭn′dərd), stole, using force; robbed by force, as in enemy raids or war.

political (pə-lĭt′ə-kəl), having to do with politics; having to do with the government or people interested in government, as a political party.

politics (pŏl′ə-tĭks), the science or practice of government; ideas about government which a person follows, as my mother's politics were for more women in government positions.

possessions (pə-zěsh′ənz), things, or property, owned by a person; territory ruled by a nation.

poverty (pŏv′ər-tĭ), the condition of being poor; without money or property or a means of making a living.

prairie (prâr′ĭ), a large stretch of usually fertile level or rolling land, with few or no trees.

prehistoric (prē′hĭs-tôr′ĭk), having to do with a time before written records were kept; having to do with a time before written history.

pressure (prĕsh′ər), the feeling of a weight pressing down; the force of one body upon the surface of another body.

proclamation (prŏk′lə-mā′shən), a public announcement, usually made by an officer of the government.

profitable (prŏf′ĭt-ə-bəl), useful; rewarding.

progress (prŏg′rĕs), growth; improvement.

progress (prə-grĕs)′, to move ahead; to go on.

prosperous (prŏs′pər-əs), successful; doing well; fortunate.

provided, given; supplied.

puzzling, hard to solve; not clear; something hard to understand.

ramrod (răm′rŏd′), a rod, or long thin metal stick, used to push powder or shot into the muzzle of a gun.

realized, understood clearly.

rear, near, at or in the back of anything.

recreational (rĕk′rĭ-ā′shən-əl), having to do with games, or play, or any relaxing amusement.

region (rē′jən), any large piece of land; a place; an area.

reliable (rĭ-lī′ə-bəl), able to be trusted; dependable.

resource (rĭ-sōrs′), a country's wealth in products, or money, or power, such as America's natural *resources*.

respect (rĭ-spĕkt′), to admire, and look up to; to honor.

responsibility (rĭ-spŏn′sə-bĭl′ə-tĭ), having a duty to; being responsible.

responsible (rĭ-spŏn′sə-bəl), reliable; worthy of being trusted; deserving either praise or blame, as the student was *responsible* for the class when the teacher left the room.

retarded (rĭ-tär′dəd), held back; slowed down.

routes (rōōts, routs), paths or roads followed in a regular way; paths used for travel.

sanitation (săn′ə-tā′shən), the ways and means of improving conditions to ensure the good health of all the people.

satellites (săt′ə-līts), small bodies that move around other and bigger bodies, such as planets; objects shot into space by men which orbit around the earth.

scarce, not very much of; rare; not easy to get or find, as the crops were *scarce* because there was no rain.

schedule (skĕj′ōōl), a timetable; a list, either written or printed, of times for doing certain things or being at certain places.

seize (sēz), to grab with force in a sudden movement; to take possession of by force, as the soldiers were ordered to *seize* the castle.

shacks, huts or cabins roughly built, or in poor condition.

shallower, less deep than; not so deep as other parts or places, as the water was *shallower* near the shore.

sickened, made ill; disgusted; became sick.

sincere (sĭn-sĭr′), honest; not false.

site, location or place of a thing, such as a building, or campgrounds.

snags, broken branches, stumps, or other parts of trees sticking up from the bottom of a stream or river; hidden obstacles.

superior (sə-pĭr′ĭ-ər), better or higher than other things or people; of higher quality; first-rate.

supplied, provided; gave what was needed; added something that was missing or needed.

suspicious (sə-spĭsh′əs), not having trust in; doubtful; thinking something is wrong or not true without having proof.

temporary (tĕm′pǝ-rĕr′ĭ), not for long; lasting only a little while.

thread, to move or go along a path carefully; to make one's way, especially in a crowd, or narrow passage, as to *thread* one's way through a mob of people, or *thread* one's way through the woods.

threatened (thrĕt′ǝnd), caused danger to; warned of trouble that might happen.

thriving, doing well; succeeding; growing rich and strong.

toil, to work long and hard at a job.

trembled, shook without control from strong feeling, such as great fear or excitement.

tremendous (trĭ-mĕn′dǝs), unusually great; very large.

trimming, clipping or cutting away to make something look neater.

tyrant (tī′rǝnt), a person who has complete power over others, and uses his power cruelly.

unusual (ŭn-ū′zhŏŏ-ǝl), out of the ordinary; extraordinary; exceptional.

vetoing (vē′tō-ĭng), in government, a president or governor refusing to sign a bill passed by the legislature, and so preventing the bill from becoming a law; refusing to agree; not permitting.

violently (vī′ǝ-lǝnt-lĭ), with great force; acting with or showing rough, strong feeling.

volunteer (vŏl′ǝn-tir′), anyone who enters a service, like the army, by his own choice; a person who offers his services free of charge, as a *volunteer* fireman or *volunteer* safety guard.

wronged, treated someone badly, or in a harmful way.

waging, fighting, or carrying on, as *waging* a war against crime.

INDEX